The Evolution of Human Consciousness and Linguistic Behavior

The Evolution of Human Consciousness and Linguistic Behavior

A Synthetic Approach to the Anthropology and Archaeology of Language Origins

Karen A. Haworth and Terry J. Prewitt

ROWMAN & LITTLEFIELD
Lanham • Boulder • New York • London

Published by Rowman & Littlefield
An imprint of The Rowman & Littlefield Publishing Group, Inc.
4501 Forbes Boulevard, Suite 200, Lanham, Maryland 20706
www.rowman.com

6 Tinworth Street, London SE11 5AL, United Kingdom

Copyright © 2020 by The Rowman & Littlefield Publishing Group, Inc.

All rights reserved. No part of this book may be reproduced in any form or by any electronic or mechanical means, including information storage and retrieval systems, without written permission from the publisher, except by a reviewer who may quote passages in a review.

British Library Cataloguing in Publication Information Available

Library of Congress Control Number: 2020940918

Library of Congress Cataloging-in-Publication Data Is Available

ISBN 978-1-5381-4288-2 (cloth)
ISBN 978-1-5381-7119-6 (pbk)
ISBN 978-1-5381-4289-9 (electronic)

In memory of Bruce Dunn, who allowed my direction to run so far afield of his work in research psychology. He was the consummate mentor, ever providing me with only the most encouraging and positive feedback.
—Karen A. Haworth

In memory of John Deely, friend and colleague over the many years, whose work helped inspire the direction of our studies.
—Terry J. Prewitt

Contents

Preface		ix
1	Beginnings	1
2	What Language Is, and Is Not	11
3	Overview of the Upper Paleolithic	23
4	Encountering Autism	31
5	Cognitive Styles	41
6	Art of the Upper Paleolithic	49
7	Empirical Corroboration	57
8	Art of the Mesolithic	67
9	Signs and Lithic Technology	77
10	The Bubble Analogy	95
11	Semiotics of Human Evolution	115
12	Finding Time	131
Index		153
About the Authors		161

Preface

The challenge of writing this book grew out of thirty years of engagement with a difficult question: How and when did humans, uniquely among all life-forms in our experience, acquire the capacity for language as we know it? The subject is a popular one, which has over the centuries also inspired detailed attention from students of many disciplines. Our intended audience will include the wide range of such scholarly specialists as well as the interested general public. We admit that a brief treatment of demanding issues does not present an "easy read." Nonetheless, in order to draw from and coordinate the disciplines of paleoanthropology, cognitive science, evolutionary biology, art history, and semiotics, a certain level of precision in terms has been necessary. The result is a novel discussion of the human achievement of language capacity, focused primarily upon the unique evolutionary developments created by a shifting balance between holistic and analytical thought. Given a choice between focused brevity versus encyclopedic treatment, we opted for a concise presentation. Given the specialized terms of the several disciplines involved, this makes for a difficult read in places, but we have balanced this tendency, we hope, with our personal narratives describing how we moved toward our understanding of issues. Since our perspective on language evolution has not heretofore received any systematic treatment, we hope that we may inspire such depth of analysis among the coming generations of scholars.

After setting down background for the problem of language origins in our first three chapters, in chapters four through eight we engage in detailed discussions of holistic cognition, considering the art and archaeology of the Paleolithic and Mesolithic periods in reference to the cognitive abilities of contemporary "visual thinkers." The concluding four chapters present arguments for both a proposed evolutionary process and documented outcomes for the expansion of human consciousness by increased emphasis of analytical or linear thinking. Throughout this book, our semiotic representation proceeds from the sign classification of American philosopher Charles Sanders Peirce. Through Peirce's categories, we provide a brief but comprehensive explanation of what prehistoric art and artifacts suggest about language origins. More importantly, our careful applications of the sign classification enhanced our ability to bridge initial conceptual differences in both analysis and writing. Our semiotic perspective also grounds an argument that iconic and indexical sign processes in hominid cognition long precede any habitual use of symbols in words or propositions, or complex narrative arguments. Through that understanding, we place the habitual use of symbols as a rapid development only after twenty thousand years ago.

Our inclusion of personal narratives intends to offer background that will help make a dense academic argument more accessible to the widest audience possible. In fact, we believe that diligent non-specialists will be able to expand their appreciation of the subject. We feel our insights into the basis of language as we know it, especially as a modeling system establishing the very flexible human worldview, has potential to clarify both popular and epistemic misconceptions in several areas of education, psychology, anthropology, prehistory, and art, to name but a few relevant disciplines. We certainly hope to inspire some colleagues toward new work, especially in recognizing holistic consciousness as deserving more attention in studies of individuals and culture.

Chapter One

Beginnings

This book presents a new perspective on an old query—the origin and evolution of human language and consciousness. The subject is one of the key questions behind the human condition, one that has been taken up time and again by hundreds of philosophers and scientists for many decades of research and contemplation. When we began our study on the subject, we made an attempt to apprise ourselves of the existing works on the issue and quickly realized the difficulty of the task, as new publications seemed to be arriving with each passing day. This is because the origin of human language remains one of those fascinating subjects that seems to be ever-present in scholarship. To understand how humans formed language is tantamount to knowing what exactly defines humanity as a separate and significant species. Discovering how and where language was derived would be nothing less than understanding how human beings came into existence.

Within this vast canon of published works, speculations are wide-ranging, each removed from the others in terms of outlook, foundational data, and basic assumptions. A few scholars have made partial steps toward a synthetic (or unifying) explanation of language origins by attempting to bring together some of these perspectives into a more cohesive whole. What we will offer here is not a comprehensive perspective, but one that is well-grounded in the evidence from many disciplines while building our argument around a single and relatively simple idea, namely: that language origins lie in a neurological transformation extending beyond the increases in brain size that mark the human evolutionary line generally and which produce the emergence of a cognitive disposition that is dominated by analytical rather than holistic thought.

While our vision of language evolution is derived from this single premise, the argument supporting it is a complex one that suggests new directions for the study of the evolution of human consciousness. We see in our analysis implications for many areas of study in the social sciences, education, and even the arts. We feel moved to present our work as a modest prompt toward greater synthesis among these fields. Consistent with the task, we have been ruminating on the overall model for a couple of decades, and we now feel our take on the subject is well-formed enough to stimulate inquiry in these other relevant fields. At the very least we hope our perspective will place the understanding of language origins in an entirely new light.

PRESENTATION THROUGH MELDING PERSPECTIVES

Our initial "simple idea" proposes that the key to understanding the evolution of language stems from the distinction in human cognition between the holistic and analytic forms of information processing. We are not introducing new concepts in cognitive studies. Holistic versus analytical thinking are established classifications in psychology and cognitive science, and this will be more thoroughly discussed in later chapters. But, simply put, it is the notion that humans take in their surroundings in two very distinct ways: either by encountering an entire field of perceptual stimuli in distinct wholes (holistic) or through noting specifics within a given experience, making comparisons, and judging contrasts from past experiences (analytic). Both modes are always present in thought but vary in their intensity across individuals. And, as an essential part of our argument, we suggest that an overarching slant toward the analytic style in *Homo sapiens sapiens* was essential for the full development of human language.

Given our rather heady goal of prompting new research directions, the task we have set for ourselves may seem outrageous. Why should we suggest the need for such a basic change in all the fields we have considered? We have not, after all, invented or discovered entirely new data. The points discussed in this book derive from many other works. But we are gathering these ideas into one argument and focusing them in such a way as to help bring some understanding to enigmatic problems that seem always to accompany language-origins discussions. In working toward a relevant synthesis of materials we have considered, we hope to contribute to an emergent new general theory of language and human origins. And, we think that the result will be useful not only to the work within any particular field but should steer or "shift" insights and directions for others.

Beyond the holistic and analytic elements of cognition derived in psychology and the cognitive sciences, many other kinds of scholarship contribute to our understanding of language origins. These include several areas of linguistics, semiotics, and art history. The subject necessarily also involves the disciplines of paleoanthropology, human paleontology, and especially the specific interpretations in archaeology of stone-tool technology and other artifacts of hominid populations from the late Pliocene through the Pleistocene and Holocene epochs (from about two million to ten thousand years ago).

We will begin our overall argument by establishing the rationale behind the importance of the concept of cognitive styles and then complete the volume with a reassessment of the data derived from the paleoanthropological record to build an account of the evolution of *Homo sapiens sapiens*, as seen through the lens of the cognitive-styles model. In addition, we will utilize the semiotic concepts of C. S. Peirce and his hierarchical system of sign categories (to be introduced in Chapter 2). The application of Peircean semiotics may seem an unnecessary philosophical burden in our argument, but we must stress that the sign categories offer a critical means of providing coherence across disciplines, as well as clarity in addressing specific elements of language functions.

Our account will also provide a perspective that (1) encompasses the recent works in the various areas of inquiry and (2) serves to coalesce what has become a vast, and therefore confusing, array of data. Theoretical perspectives are more easily established in the infancy of a discipline where the data to be aligned are limited in scope. However, we are now "blessed" with a multitude of what can seem to be conflicting facts that demand a more comprehensive basis for analysis. For instance, while the early hominid record has stressed mainly African sites, the later interpretations of the genus Homo have reflected distinctively Eurocentric and sometimes Asian biases. Our synthesis of hominid evolution recognizes the emergence of the early Upper Paleolithic of South Africa, at least some sixty-five thousand years ago. Work related to this African Upper Paleolithic seems critical, to us at least, for the reinterpretation of the Middle and Upper Paleolithic of Europe, the Near East, Asia, and Australia. Indeed, any comprehensive theory of origins involving *Homo erectus* and *Homo sapiens* "stages" of development, including the plethora of other named populations, must take into account all of the data from the diverse regions and time periods. There are several extant interpretations of the record, each with quite different implications with regard to the language problem (for traditional and recent syntheses, see Brantingham, Kuhn, and Kerry 2004; Aiello and Dunbar 1993; Cunliffe 1994; Shreeve 1995). We use these in developing our general view of the evolutionary process for human cognition.

In any event, an array of geographically and temporally distinct fossil forms is loosely aligned with technological evidence, with only subtle physiological features in the fossil record through which to suggest cognitive developments. Fortunately, some elements of general mammalian comparative anatomy and ontogeny are very helpful in setting the stage for interpretations of both initial and subsequent hominid development. We have attempted here to follow the main transformations at each stage of change, introducing relevant empirical supports for new capacities. In this way, we can present a clearer argument for what happened at each stage while also understanding the novel elements within the larger ground of diversity. The process we describe, then, is one of emergent imminent abilities, their incorporation into the behavioral repertoires of daily life, and the conditions that follow for subsequent changes.

Our general approach in presenting our argument is to keep the discussion as non-technical as possible, in the interest of providing non-specialists a solid background for accessing the complete argument, while using references and notes to elaborate on technical details. But the problem requires an even broader approach and depth of inquiry, the assimilation of myriad apparently unrelated things into a unified perspective. Happily, our current technology and systems of scholarly sharing make such work less daunting, especially for researchers who bring special expertise alongside an openness to share across academic boundaries. No single perspective can tackle the question, and probably no single explanation will ever offer a comprehensive answer. But we are closer today to knowing how we came to be, how speech evolved, how we gained the capacity to "know," and what the general process has meant for humanity.

PRESENTATION THROUGH NARRATIVE

Another aspect of presentation for our argument on language origins, as seen through the lens of cognitive styles, is that it will be introduced in part through personal narrative. This is because narrative is central to analytical thinking, in general. This mode of thought is often referred to in academic literature as linear or sequential thinking. That is because, when people attempt to make sense of our surroundings, we tend to see things as one event following another, as in the flow of events in time. This analytical aspect involves the notion that one thing possibly causes the next—the basic underlying element of any problem-solving activity. "If I do this, then this occurs as a result." Seeing causal relationships between elements in our surroundings is basic to our thought process and usually serves us well (though, of course, spurious interconnections are also rampant in our thinking).

For the most part, analytical thought works to provide us with problem solutions and has been a key basis for human information gathering from our beginning. But the serial aspect has also been our favored method of recording and conveying knowledge, hence the ubiquitous characteristic of myth, story, and folktales that permeates all cultures—the narrative. Unfortunately, the analytic bias became so pervasive in Western culture that the interrelations between events became paramount over story, and narrative as a means of imparting our knowledge base became lost in our Age of "Enlightenment." We placed the word here in quotes to suggest the "air quotes" used in conversation that denotes the ironic aspect of the term enlightenment. For although our scientific revolution brought about marvels of human ingenuity, there was also something lost in the dry and staid records of academia. A little of humanity gets lost when scientific works fail to relate back in some way to the human condition as it unfolds or, more importantly, to the general public audience. This is particularly necessary within the social sciences, where we are seeking to understand humanity in general.

That is why we have always valued those academic authors who honestly placed themselves into the surroundings they studied instead of establishing a pretense (which is all it can be) of an uninvolved observer. Hence, the ongoing writing of our ethnographic work on Irish culture is presented through poetry and short story along with hard demographic and economic data and our "scientific" arguments. Indeed, in much of our individual writing leading up to this volume, we have employed the forms of narrative and poetry in casting our philosophical views (for example, see: Prewitt 2015 and 2009; Haworth 2006). Such "messy" texts (a technical term within the ethnographic and literary fields) are becoming more common in academic discourse, enabling the reader to both deduce meaning and better understand the narrator as a source of knowledge.

We apply something similar in this volume as well, centering around the certain *coincidental* experiences that brought us to this particular treatment of the origins of language. Along the way throughout this book, we will periodically establish particular points of our argument as they arose in our thinking and as the story unfolded in time through various events in our academic lives. When it becomes necessary to introduce background material that also guided our thoughts, these points will be presented in a more traditional form. We consider the overall flow of events and ideas to be significant and important to the development of our argument, and so we have chosen to keep them in our narrative, to keep ourselves in the story, and to provide our audience a grounding element and possibly a better means of judgment of our process. Indeed, the shifts from narrative to explanatory modes of expression mirror the process we have gone through in gaining a mutual understanding of the problems at hand and their solution. Although our argument, in the end, is a traditional one, it rests upon a much more complex foundation of disparate experiences.

Karen's Story: As noted earlier, our approach to the evolution of language stems from work in a number of different fields of scientific inquiry. But it also derives from some chance occurrences that led us to delve into these areas outside our primary fields. It has taken me several decades to recognize the importance of these serendipitous elements to our research, but I have also recently come to realize that these events would not have been significant to most others. They were important to my husband and me because of our particular academic backgrounds that made a multidisciplinary approach to this problem possible.

Both Terry and I are generalists in the widest sense of the term, first because our primary academic background is in anthropology. This field is also multifaceted in its very definition, with four primary subdisciplines: archaeology, ethnology, physical anthropology, and linguistics. Not only are anthropologists expected to have foundational knowledge of all these areas, in spite of individual specializations, we each have chosen to maintain a strong involvement in all of the areas at the advanced levels of our education. Terry has worked professionally as an archaeologist and a cultural anthropologist, while most of his published works over the years are in textual analysis and semiotics (expanding on his background in linguistics). And, his professorship in a small university meant several years of teaching general courses including physical anthropology and culture history in his department. My postgraduate work was nominally in psychology, but the program I took up was an interdisciplinary one in cognitive science. This meant background courses in counseling psychology, research psychology, and education and learning research, in addition to expanding on my anthropological studies. My interest in this program was, from the outset, centered around the evolution of language, and my studies focused on the various language experiments of the mid-twentieth century, particularly those involving attempts to introduce human communication systems to other species, especially other primate species. In the end, once our kernel theory on language evolution was developed, our subsequent research involved simply refining our existing basic knowledge in all these fields. Noting this generalized academic experience is important for understanding the extent to which I was thoroughly primed, so to speak, to interpret the first of our chance occurrences in the way I did.

This first serendipitous experience dates from the mid-1980s when Terry and I were doing ethnographic work in Ireland. Our first few months were spent in Dublin, with Terry teaching at University College and conducting background demographic research there for our later ethnographic work in the western county of Clare. My contribution to the project was to provide the photographic and cartographic record for the research once we were set up in Clare, so my primary responsibility in the city was domestic, as our toddler daughter was also accompanying us on this research trip.

Being located in an apartment in Dublin for three months provided us delightful access to British, as well as Irish, television programing. During this time frame the BBC was at its heyday in providing educational fare during the daytime hours, and so I happened on a documentary looking at the phenomenon of artistic talent discovered within the population of autistic children. The program documented one of the seminal studies on autism by Lorna Selfe (1977). At that point in time the syndrome was relatively newly classified and also still considered a very rare condition (though the rise in rates of autism in recent decades has made this a now commonplace diagnosis).

The documentary centered on the drawing talents of one particular child, "Nadia." The drawings presented in the program, from when Nadia was only five and six years old, were quite impressive and made for good television. The unusual style of the drawings was loose and flowing and full of movement, reminiscent to me of a Michelangelo sketch, or at least an adult artist. They were definitely not the simple single-line drawings common to most children.

Nadia's drawings also centered primarily around animal subjects, and their naturalism was doubly impressive, since: (1) she had little direct experience with the animals she drew, but interpreted from static and elementary illustrations from a coloring book; and (2) she had no prior experience with the drawing medium. Her impressive works dated from the very first time she put pencil to paper at the age of five.

For me, the unusual animal depictions brought to mind another body of enigmatic art found in the caves of the Upper Paleolithic. As an anthropologist, I was, of course, quite familiar with the impressive, yet unexplained artworks discovered in the caves of southern France and northern Spain that had made good news stories for decades, as they continue to do today. The phenomenon of sophisticated representations appearing with apparently no precursor development has challenged the academic community from the time of their initial discovery in the nineteenth century. And like the language-origins question, these artworks have served to inspire countless studies and volumes of surmises and conjectures on them.

For me the similarities of the two bodies of work provided the kernel idea behind my future research: Could there be some underlying connection between the natural and untrained visual talents of this autistic child, who incidentally did not develop speech without intense training, and the equally impressive works of early Homo sapiens, dating from a time with no apparent evidence for language capability?

This was an interesting question, but it remained one of idle curiosity for several years. During this time Terry resumed teaching duties stateside and began work on a monograph on our Irish research and other writing in linguistic analysis. I worked as administrative support staff for the art department at the same university and had progressed to the thesis level on my degree in cognitive science. My observational research on early psychological development of a chimpanzee at a local zoo had stalled. This was supposed to provide me with some data on the natural cognitive development of another primate species, observed without any of the research interference inherent to the ape language experiments. I wanted to establish a better baseline of behavior that was largely lacking in the record on these works. However, I found that working with a solitary *individual could not provide a natural or realistic record of development of a very social species, and I dropped the project.*

Meanwhile, my time spent working with artists at the university actually helped to ground my eventual research into our theory of language evolution. I didn't realize it at the time, but my experiences working with the visually minded artists, in contrast to the analytic thinkers in anthropology and semiotics, helped my understanding of the visual cognitive mode soon to be a new extension of my language-evolution research.

Also, my time discussing early art history with the students and colleagues in that department served to keep my kernel idea alive. Eventually, through substantial conversation and discussion, I was convinced that maybe this idea was worthy of further study. I decided I would broach the possibility of a change of tactic for my thesis work with my mentor in the psychology department, Bruce Dunn. He was concerned about my stalled research and welcomed my idea of the change. My work would now center on theoretical issues instead of experimental observation. In order to progress along these lines, I began to look more closely at the archaeological record of the Upper Paleolithic, deferring for a while broader evolutionary issues, and then comparing the archaeological data to the psychological record on autism.

As I pursued my thesis, Terry and I began to discuss the nature of language. Ultimately, we came to view language through the work of American semiotic scholars following C. S. Peirce, as opposed to linguistic specialists whose views of semiotics were grounded in the work of Ferdinand de Saussure. But at that early time, we found ourselves at odds on our perspectives toward the basic concepts underlying the notion of language, given an early structuralist bias on Terry's part. Our conflict was ultimately resolved in favor of Peircean semiotics, which progressively provided critical breakthroughs in our handling of the diverse subject matters in our long-term research. Before going deeply into the progress of my thesis, then, in this work we want to present a statement on concepts of language as we understand them today, and that is the subject of our next chapter.

WORKS CITED

Aiello, L. C., and R. I. M. Dunbar. 1993. "Neocortex Size, Group Size, and the Evolution of Language." *Current Anthropology* 34: 2.

Brantingham, Steven, L. Kuhn, and Kristopher W. Kerry. 2004. *The Early Upper Paleolithic beyond Western Europe*. Berkeley: University of California Press.

Cunliffe, B. 1994. *The Oxford Illustrated Prehistory of Europe*. Oxford: Oxford University Press.

Haworth, Karen A. 2006. "Cognitive Style and Zoosemiotics." In *Semiotics 2004/2005: Proceedings of the Thirtieth Annual Meeting of the Semiotic Society of America*, edited by Stacy Monahan, Benjamin Smith, and Terry Prewitt, 78–87. New York: Legas Publishing.

Prewitt, Terry J. 2015. "Why Semiotics, Why Poetry." In *Semiotica* 2015, Issue 207, 443–50. ISSN (Online) 1613-3692, ISSN (Print) 0037-1998, https://doi.org/10.1515/sem-2015-0059.

———. 2009. "Poetics and Peirce: The Semiotics of Spiraling Meaning." In *Semiotics 2008*, edited by John Deely, 904–10. New York: Legas Press.

Selfe, Lorna. 1977. *Nadia: A Case of Extraordinary Drawing Ability in an Autistic Child*. London: Academic Press.

Shreeve, J. 1995. *The Neanderthal Enigma: The Mystery of Modern Human Origins*. New York: William Morrow and Company, Inc.

Chapter Two

What Language Is, and Is Not

People talk. This is the comfortable certainty of our existence that sets us apart from all the other animals. Of course, animals also communicate, but not in our distinctively human way. In possessing the gift of speech, we are alone. And yet we know today that we are inextricably connected to the rest of the living world; there is only one basis for the living organisms on our planet, DNA, and we share in that. With other primates, our heritage is shared in very substantial ways.

A natural question arises, then, which has never been satisfactorily answered: How did our evolutionary lineage acquire from the many capacities we share with other species the unique combination of elements supporting language?

The "how" question is primary, since it entails the "when" and "where" of the problem. To repeat what bears repeating, the "problem" of language origins involves the combined information from a host of independent disciplines—linguistics, paleoanthropology, cognitive science, evolutionary biology, and even such diverse fields as aesthetics and ethology. What, then, is the best starting point for defining what we mean by "language"? Indeed, before we can address the question of "how," we should be clear on what exactly "language" includes, what it excludes, and how we can recognize it when we encounter it.

Some might ask, "Can the definition of language be that difficult?" Yet, there has been a lot of ink spilled to muddy that question over the past fifty years, and the most-reasoned voices have not always been given the most popular play. Science is not immune to being pushed by popular interests and misconceptions, and there is the added difficulty that we must use language to explain any sense of language. In the current case, the issue has become one of whether, or to what extent, our closest animal kin among the great apes (or sometimes other species) share in the abilities we call language. There is also the element of our individual involvements with these issues over time, and so we will first engage that story through a personal narrative we feel best sets the context for what follows.

Terry's Story: As I was completing my doctoral dissertation, while also teaching at the University of Tulsa, well before Karen became engaged in her interest in language origins, I was already deeply interested in linguistic issues as they related to the study of culture. I was fortunate to have mentors who had studied with Kenneth Pike, as well as several who had worked with Julian Steward and were more inclined to the orientation of cultural materialism following the writings of Marvin Harris. I also personally had some influential direct experience with both Kenneth Pike and Marvin Harris. This was standard background for many in my generation of anthropologists, and I wrote and presented papers grounded in both structural linguistics and materialist cultural history. Since my schooling was pursued through the University of Oklahoma, I also had various contacts in Norman, Oklahoma, that ultimately touched on the interests of this book. I enjoyed a friendship with Roger Fouts, whose work with the signing chimpanzee Washoe was prominent at the time, and even was present at some of the early graduate presentations of Sue Savage-Rumbaugh, who went on to diverse major studies of primate language capabilities. My own thinking about the chimpanzee language experiments was influenced by Roger, especially as I had opportunities to observe some of his work firsthand. At the same time, I was skeptical of the natural abilities of the higher primates, though at that time I had no theoretical rubric through which to express those reservations.

In 1981, quite by chance at a meeting of the American Anthropological Association, I met Michael Herzfeld, who was at that point the assistant director of the Semiotics Institute at Indiana University. Through Michael I also met another mentor, Thomas A. Sebeok, director of that institute and the primary figure in the semiotic revival in American academia—a revival that drew together scholars from such diverse fields as philosophy, anthropology, literary studies, architecture, mathematics, art history, and many other disciplines. This was the beginning of my involvement in semiotics, which remained my focus throughout my entire professional career.

As Karen was beginning her formal work on language origins, I was also already closely associated with John Deely, working with him in the administration of the Semiotic Society of America, supporting the work of other scholars with similar interests and becoming even more thoroughly "generalist" in my studies than I had been within the canopy of anthropology. Every connection of my academic life prepared me, in one way or another, to pursue the questions of this book. Still, for a number of years I remained essentially "structuralist" and then "post-structuralist" in my theoretical grounding, eschewing the treacherous marsh of Peircean philosophy for what seemed a less esoteric approach to sign theory. There were many steps in my eventual adoption of the Peircean categories as a framework for understanding experience. Early on, my linguistic bias presented little difficulty in my discussions with Karen on language issues, but as her work progressed it was increasingly apparent that we were often talking past each other. The difficulty was not her psychological bias so much as my formal linguistic one. In fact, I had little influence on the conceptualization or completion of her thesis on language origins, leaving that entirely to her mentor, Bruce Dunn.

So, how did we bridge that gap in understanding? The process became more intense when Floyd Merrell (2007) published a short paper espousing Peircean semiotics as an essential ground for understanding, which Karen (Haworth 2009) followed with an essay of her own. In reading these essays, I began to reorganize my thinking, working closely with my student and colleague Robert Philen, who was more well-versed in philosophy than I, assimilating what I knew, or thought I knew, into the formal sign categories of Charles S. Peirce. The benefit of this was a common framework through which Karen and I could discuss our individual perspectives and ultimately the theoretical grounding for approaching all of the backgrounds involved in our collaborative writing. This was a personal paradigm shift that for both of us underpins the current work.

APES, HUMANS, AND PEIRCEAN SIGN CATEGORIES

Given the information gained through extensive studies in primate communication, there is now no question that our ape cousins use sophisticated signs, not only in captivity but also in natural settings (for instance, see Lancaster 1975; Patterson and Linden 1981; Goodall 1986; Fouts 1997; Savage-Rumbaugh, Shanker, and Taylor 1998). Fortunately, we have ample observations to compare how humans and apes use signs, and the results of such a comparison become very relevant for the broader question of language origins. Ironically, as we shall see, the demonstration of how apes are not like us in the use of signs confirms how very closely we are related in evolutionary terms, providing also grist for better interpretations of the record of prehistoric hominids from *Australopithecus* through *Homo sapiens*.

However, how should we classify and compare sign capacities? The answer to that question was offered in the nineteenth century by the American philosopher Charles Sanders Peirce (1867, 1868, 1868a).[1] His thoughtful explorations of signifying behaviors helped ground our contemporary field of semiotics and more directly provided a set of explicit terms for the analysis of signs wherever they might occur. From the later work of scholars Thomas Sebeok (1976), John Deely (1994), and many others, we also know that signs are used widely in the animal kingdom, so the evolutionary connection of animal and human communication systems runs throughout most of the history of life on our planet.

The most important idea from which to embark on a discussion of Peirce's classification is the recognition that experience through signs applies to all life-forms, if it is not in fact "the" grounding feature of our biological universe. What many people today mean when they use the term "sign" is, in the Peircean classification, a "symbol," to such an extent that the terms are often used interchangeably. However, symbols are a rather specific and high-level phenomenon within the realm of "something representing something to someone." Grounding the "symbol" is an array of other ways that the world is experienced, ranging from an appreciation of the mere quality of differences in things around us, through more complex constructions of difference as discrete phenomena, to the ultimate selection of meaningful constructions that guide behavior. Peirce organized the elements of signification into a system involving three sets of distinctions: (1) what the sign is as an object of apprehension, (2) what the sign is as something that represents its object, and (3) what the sign means in a specific instance of its use. These three elements (object, representamen, and interpretant) are further differentiated in terms of three sets of three distinctions. Although we do not belabor the terms of the classification in every part of this book, our readers should be aware that we use the classification very precisely as a basis for our work, and so we are introducing the nomenclature here.[2]

At the base of the classification, the *qualisign* involves an appreciation of "some difference" as distinguished from the background of all experience. It is contrasted to the *sinsign*, an appreciation that becomes relevant to its user, and the *legisign*, an appreciation of regularities or patterns in the surrounding world. Since some of the sign process underlying any *semiosis* (the ongoing experience of the world through signs) is unconscious, it is common to distinguish the species-specific experience of the world, or *umwelt*, from what we think of as the "actively experienced" or sometimes "constructed" world, or *lebenswelt*, drawing from distinctions common in philosophy and semiotics (for a good basic examination of the two concepts, see Deely, 1990, 1994). The basic idea is that there are sign processes active in semiosis that are never brought to the surface of sense or perception and many kinds of sinsigns and legisigns that are never brought into conscious expression. Further, much of animal behavior can be understood as a demonstration of uniqueness or regularity experienced though these basic sign processes.

In concert with these distinctions, semiotic explanations recognize that every species has biologically determined capacities that limit or define what can be experienced directly, and how, and also, what can be brought into the lived world in ways that can modify or define behavior. The closer two species are phylogenetically, the more similar will be their respective potentials. For example, a chimpanzee and a human share much in their basic biological capacities, as also suggested by purely physiological comparisons. But we should never presume that two species have identical experiences of what is outside them. Nor can we even presume experiential agreement within two individuals of the same species. In the end, observed behavior may underscore major differences in what appear to be closely related species. Thus, to stay with the current example, a chimpanzee and bonobo, for all their gross morphological similarity, are quite different animals with very different "semiosic" repertoires.

Moving beyond the first triad of the Peircean view, we encounter the *icon*, *index*, and *symbol*. The *icon* is a sign that represents through similarity with its object—an image, a map, a diagram, and on some levels, a metaphor. This is contrasted to the *index*, which represents by juxtaposition in the moment—pointing, in essence. The word pointing, however, is somewhat misleading, since smoke can serve as an index to fire. Or fever *points* to a variation from the normal state of body temperature. Indeed, much of the foundation of semiotics was created in the area of medicine, where the study of "symptoms" is essentially the study of indices. Index signs are not so connected to specific objects as are icons, but they are very versatile in handling a myriad of situations where a map or comparison is of little value. A behavior indicating "danger" need not be specific, though it *may* be; all that is important is that the sign register some potential, or some looming possibility. The *symbol*, finally, is a sign that refers to something by convention, as we shall show in more detail below.

It should be clear that the Peircean categories are not necessarily mutually exclusive. A sign may be an icon and an index at the same time, or as in the case of a road sign that says "danger," simultaneously a symbol. But the symbol, as we shall see, represents through conventional agreement. There is nothing in the symbol that gives a clue as to what is being represented, save the commonly experienced association that users of the symbol have assimilated and more or less agree upon. But the symbol is more complex than that, and deserves a fuller elaboration, as we also continue to the last three elements of Peirce's classification.

SYMBOLS

How does Peircean subclassification of signs help differentiate human language from ape communication? The answer to this question lies in a division Peirce created within the overall classification. He introduced a division among *terms*, *propositions*, and *arguments* (or, rhemes, dicents, and arguments). This cross-cutting set of philosophical distinctions, which in the case of human language essentially yields words, inferences, and explanations, is partly shared by many other species. Peirce and other semiotic scholars have used a variety of other ways of expressing the difference, but the gist of all of the discussions is the same. Individual symbols or "terms" carry with them a set of basic associations that can be very simple or complex, as in the differences between the words "black" or "fire" (the simple) and "DNA" or "epistemology" (the complex). In language, this basic symbol can be recognized as the "word" (or in technical linguistic terms, the "morph"). When two terms are connected logically, however, as with "smoke indexing fire," the result is essentially an "if/then" proposition, and this is the basis of the second kind of "symbol" recognized by Peirce. The third involves combining many terms and propositions to offer an explanation or argument about the world, for example all of the associations of experience that explain something like "burning," or "cooking," or more to the present point, "the origin and evolution of language."

Both ape behavior and human language bring into focus the symbol, understood by Peirce as always involving some kind of "conventional" or "shared" use beyond the individual. It should be noted that what symbols accomplish is an arbitrary codification of the non-symbolic signs that an individual mind may experience or manifest. We may note that the word "fire" represents a specific collection of qualitative experiences of heat, flame, smoke, and so on, raised from the level of mere sense (sinsigns) to a recognized regularity (legisign). As a symbol, the word "fire" constitutes an arbitrary convention of English, which has other rough counterparts in other human languages. However, the understanding of smoke as an index of fire is a "natural" proposition (or *dicent* sign, discussed below) that can be learned by experience, and that may be integrated into the appreciation of the sign itself. When we humans see smoke and call out "fire!" we are using the symbol to indicate the proposition. This is true even if the caller has not seen actual fire. When the proposition is further understood as "danger," that is also an extension of learned associations. But such signs can be shared without being symbolic, as with the flicking of a squirrel's tail as an index of danger directed in general, which is neither "conventional" nor "arbitrary," but biologically encoded in the squirrel's behavior. And further, many experiential non-symbolic terms and propositions occur widely in the animal world, and especially among the primates under study here.

Among sign categories, the symbol simply requires that two individuals construct and recognize more or less the same *arbitrary* basis for representing some interpretation of the world. The symbol, then, is a consequence of learning at some level. The "more or less" aspect of the sharing is critical, since for the individual there is no guarantee of perfect harmony with the constructions and associations of others. This point cannot be overstressed and will be reiterated throughout this volume. The meaning of a symbol, then, must be deduced from its context and potential consequences of usage, visible and observable in the surrounding world. The boy who cried "Wolf!" was calling out danger, but eventually others turned the interpretation of the call in a different direction. Ultimately, an assertion is never confirmed by mere convention, but by its repeated consequences. Even so, the meaning of a symbol in the here and now is always a variant determined by its context. Since the symbol employs arbitrary means of expression, it can be a very effective shorthand for much more complex conditions, and in that sense receives emphasis in our argument about the evolution of language capacity (see Chapter 10).

From a Peircean perspective, we should understand that fifty years of "ape language" research has demonstrated a capacity among orangutans, gorillas, chimps, and bonobos for captive and natural use of terms and propositions in the iconic and indexical sense, and also, at least with human intervention, in the symbolic sense. But the same research also clearly falsifies the hypothesis that the great apes or any other species can construct complex symbolic arguments. Without "the argument," there can be no Descartes or Nietzsche, and indeed, not even a discussion (which requires a rule-based system of communication) about how to cook breakfast.[3] Even so, there have been tantalizing examples of multi-propositional constructions from apes involved in sign-language experiments. Most notably, the chimpanzee Washoe combined person/place/action propositions in some of her communications with researchers.[4] The ape language experiments do suggest the need to consider pushing the origins of the capacity for symbolling back to at least the very beginnings of the Hominoidea (great apes and humans), and certainly to the beginnings of the hominid lineages. As an outside example, whale "songs" may be symbolic at least in the sense of rhemes or dicents. This observation underscores the idea that the *symbolic argument*, and not *symbol use* in its more basic forms, marks our species as different from all other animals, including the great apes. In any event, no other species has been demonstrated to possess "the argument" *as we experience it*, nor are we likely to ever encounter in our biological system another being with such sentience.

Language as we know it depends upon the ability to create symbols and manipulate them logically, of course, but that ability goes well beyond the basic symbolic behaviors we share with the apes. Humans can model the world in very complex ways using the medium of language, and in this sense language surpasses the functions of a communication system. Moreover, the evolution of logic via symbols was, at its foundation, a process supporting communication, both as enhancements to learning by imitation and for immediate needs of cooperation. Signing apes have learned symbols by imitation and training and used the learned systems with each other, but have shown, in spite of a few occasional instances, little natural tendency to create or embellish them with each other. Instead, they sign primarily with human keepers to gain food or other advantages, or to ask contextually immediate questions. This is sophisticated communication across species, but it in no way suggests that these animals have the same capacity as humans to extend their logic into symbolic modeling. Ape communication behaviors merely express iconic recognitions of pattern and indexical behaviors they already possess and share with most reptilian and mammalian species.

Remember, though, that the complex modeling of the human species is only one portion of our experiential lives, while most other aspects of our experience lie within those sign relations we share with other animals. This also cannot be overstated, and it is important to the overall message we are offering here.

SYMBOLLING AND LANGUAGE IN HOMINID EVOLUTION

In considering the evolution of language in our hominid lineage, we must recognize at least two stages in development. First, the natural emergence and adoption of symbols to express conventional referents—for example, ideas attached to morphs—and secondarily the emergence and development of internal or expressed modeling *through the habitual use of symbols*. We should note that each of these steps should also be reflected in particular material consequences—tangible elements that can be observed in the archaeological record. We suggest that the recognition of archaeological "types" by researchers is always an exploration of iconic or indexical signs, an essentially semiotic activity about "pattern semiosis" in the past. Even so, we should also take into account that such evidence may not be clearly manifest or universal across the very scattered and temporally diverse record, rich though our experience of hominid prehistory may be. Second, we should not presume that when we can see and express a pattern in the archaeological record, such a pattern suggests that the hominids responsible for the record saw their world in an identical way. Some patterns are sufficiently ubiquitous, or sufficiently different from what came before, that they cannot be denied, as with the Acheulean "axe" or the Solutrean "blade." There are, however, instances in the interpretation of hominid technology that demonstrably overreach, as we will elaborate later, for example in much of the Mousterian tool typology and some of the "reduction" process patterns of the Middle Paleolithic (see Wargo 2009; Dibble 1995).

The natural emergence of symbols and their manipulation involved changes in cognitive processes resulting from changes in the physiological systems supporting cognition—the sensory and perception elements of the central nervous system. We know today that there are many common developmental stages in general primate cognition, and that these stages reflect the "ontogeny" or developmental structure from creation of a zygote through death. The life span comprises cellular specializations beginning in earliest fetal existence, sense-responsive learning in changing chemical and structural environments of uterine and infantile life, growth changes of childhood, hormonal changes of puberty, and additional systematic alterations through adulthood into senility, and over much of the life span modulations and limitations produced by cultural behaviors. Such processes and stages are similar, but not identical, in the different primate species and can in some cases be understood in terms of specific scientifically observable patterns, "triggers" and behavioral transformations.

The emergence of a capacity for symbolic modeling presents a much more difficult problem, relying upon comparisons of capacities of different species represented or suggested by the fossil record. This is complicated by the fact that behavioral interpretations from physiological or technological clues are by no means as reliable in the Paleolithic record as would be the systematic interpretation of behaviors from artifacts "in situ" on discrete living floors. In spite of many recent advances in the methods of archaeological interpretation, we simply lack the kinds of sites that allow for such more direct behavioral reconstructions in the Pliocene and early Pleistocene. In addition, it is clear that projections back from living primates are not entirely satisfactory, since modern species are *all* "derived" (or evolved) from more generalized species within the hominoid lineages. It is difficult to assess how similar or different any australopithecine was from any modern African hominoid ape, or how generalized australopithecine capacities contributed to later hominid forms, including humans. We are on firmer ground simply comparing the various australopithecine forms. In any event, some of the differences between modern apes and humans occurred earlier, in the less well-documented populations of the dryopithecines, so we should not expect that modern apes offer precise analogies with *Australopithecus*. Fortunately, much of the story of "language" emergence occurs after *Australopithecus*, and (we suggest) some key developments occurred in the relatively comfortable eras of the late Pleistocene and early Holocene, and clearly within the complex emergence of the genus *Homo*.

Overall, the fundamental shift from the use of symbols as direct "referents to experienced phenomena" to use of symbols as "a modeling system" can be seen first in the technological expression of patterned tool industries, and later in the expression of "styles"—especially geographically divergent styles. The shift is most clear with the emergence of aesthetic and narrative capacities *within* our genus, as well as in the emergence of inscribed symbols, and ultimately writing. These are the material artifacts bearing on language origins. We may also emphasize both (1) the foundational biological capacities of symbol use across the Primate order and (2) structured evidence of extant symbolic systems, as they occur at various times past and present. So, modern ape and reconstructed early hominid abilities are certainly relevant as a ground for approaching the problem of what *language is as a communication system*. However, what we know of linguistic structure and history in modern studies presents an essentially artifactual evidence of human consciousness. In our view, then, working from that evidence, the key evolutionary event rests in the rise of *language as a modeling system*, which remains an essentially "human" story.

NOTES

1. The semiotic notes of C. S. Peirce are widely scattered in his immense corpus of writing, though the most useful for our purposes here are Peirce 1867, 1868, and 1868a in Burks (1958), "Bibliography of the Works of Charles Sanders Peirce." See also Thomas A. Sebeok (1976) and John N. Deely (1994), as well as other specific notations on Peirce throughout this book.

2. For a detailed introduction to Peirce's classification of signs and sign processes, see Corrington (1993); for briefer presentations and applications, see also Prewitt (2009), Parmentier (1994), and Chapter 9, this volume.

3. Chimpanzees have recently been suggested to possess the "patience" required for the activity of cooking, and evidently a preference for cooked food. They have yet to show any capacity to construct and communicate any recipes.

4. As with the sign construction, "LYN + WASHOE go ride car //index small plane visible from car in which Washoe and Lyn Miles were riding//" (personal communication with Lyn Miles). There are many other such examples, always context specific and limited by syntactic interpretation of the researcher, but nonetheless propositional. For example, when visiting Washoe in Oklahoma, I was wearing a cap, and Washoe signed "Give Cap" while indexing me as I entered the room.

WORKS CITED

Burks, Arthur W. 1958. "Bibliography of the Works of Charles Sanders Peirce." In *The Collected Papers of Charles Sanders Peirce*, Vol. VIII, edited by A. W. Burks, 249–330. Cambridge, MA: Harvard University Press.

Corrington, Robert S. 1993. *An Introduction to C. S. Peirce: Philosopher, Semiotician, and Ecstatic Naturalist*. Lanham, MD: Rowman & Littlefield.

Deely, John N. 1990. *Basics of Semiotics*. Bloomington: Indiana University Press.

———. 1994. *The Human Use of Signs, or Elements of Anthroposemiosis*. Lanham, MD: Rowman & Littlefield.

Dibble, H. L. 1995. "Middle Paleolithic Scraper Reduction: Background, Clarification, and Review of the Evidence to Date." *Journal of Archaeological Method and Theory* 2: 299–368.

Fouts, Roger. 1997. *Next of Kin: What Chimpanzees Have Taught Me about Who We Are*. New York: William Morrow and Company, Inc.

Goodall, Jane. 1986. *The Chimpanzees of Gombe: Patterns of Behavior*. Cambridge, MA: Belknap Press of Harvard University Press.

Haworth, Karen A. 2009. "Perceiving Peirce: Or Why I Believe Becoming a Peircean Is Necessary." In *Semiotics 2008: Proceedings of the 33rd Annual Meeting of the Semiotic Society of America*, edited by John N. Deely and Leonard Sbrocchi. New York: Legas Publishing.

Lancaster, Jane B. 1975. *Primate Behavior and the Emergence of Human Culture*. New York: Holt, Rinehart and Winston.

Merrell, Floyd. 2007. "Why I Believe Becoming a Peircean Is Preferable." *Signs* 1: 1–28 [not to be confused with the feminist journal *Signs*; the online semiotic journal *Signs* is no longer available, but the essay is in the library of the authors].

Parmentier, Richard. 1994. *Signs in Society: Studies in Semiotic Anthropology*. Bloomington: Indiana University Press.

Patterson, Francine, and Eugene Linden. 1981. *The Education of Koko*. New York: Holt, Rinehart and Winston.

Peirce, Charles S. 1867. "On a New List of Categories." In *The Collected Papers of Charles Sanders Peirce* (CP 1.545-559, chronology of A. W. Burks, 261), edited by Charles Hartshorne and Paul Weiss. Cambridge, MA: Harvard University Press. Also in *Writings of Charles S. Peirce: A Chronological Edition, Volume 2, 1867–1871*, edited by Edward Moore et al. (1984), 49–59. Bloomington: Indiana University Press.

———. 1867a. "On the Natural Classification of Arguments." In *Writings of Charles S. Peirce: A Chronological Edition, Volume 2, 1867–1871*, edited by Edward Moore et al. (1984), 23–48. Bloomington: Indiana University Press.

———. 1868. "Questions Concerning Certain Faculties Claimed for Man." *The Journal of Speculative Philosophy* 2: 103–14; reprinted in *The Collected Papers of Charles Sanders Peirce* (CP 5.264-317, chronology of A. W. Burks, 261), edited by Charles Hartshorne and Paul Weiss. Cambridge, MA: Harvard University Press.

———. 1868a. "Some Consequences of Four Incapacities." (CP 5.264-317, chronology of A. W. Burks, 261), *The Journal of Speculative Philosophy* 2: 140–57; reprinted in *The Collected Papers of Charles Sanders Peirce* (CP 5.264-317, chronology of A. W. Burks, 261), edited by Charles Hartshorne and Paul Weiss. Cambridge, MA: Harvard University Press.

Prewitt, Terry J. 2009. "The Peircean Sign-Field and Dynamics of Semiosis." In *Semiotics 2009: The Semiotics of Time*, edited by Karen A. Haworth, Jason Hogue, and Leonard G. Sbrocchi, 338–53. New York: Legas Publishing.

Savage-Rumbaugh, Sue, Stuart G. Shanker, and Talbot J. Taylor. 1998. *Apes, Language and the Human Mind*. New York: Oxford University Press.

Sebeok, Thomas A. 1976. *Contributions to the Doctrine of Signs*. Bloomington: Indiana University Press.

Wargo, Melissa Canady. 2009. *The Bordes-Binford Debate: Transatlantic Interpretive Traditions in Paleolithic Archaeology*. Doctoral dissertation: The University of Texas at Arlington. https://uta-ir.tdl.org/uta-ir/bitstream/handle/10106/1766/Wargo_uta_2502D_10351.pdf?sequence=1.

Chapter Three

Overview of the Upper Paleolithic

Karen's Story: When I first set out in my background research for the thesis project, I knew that I must at the outset confirm my initial ideas regarding the significance of the Upper Paleolithic. I spent only a modicum of time on this because I found, with only a cursory search of the record, ample material in support of its importance within the sequence of human evolution. Just through sheer numbers, the era stands out. Few time periods in our remote past have provided us with such a wealth of sites and material goods from which to glean information.

Since my initial work was rather perfunctory, we realized we needed to provide a much more thorough background for this book project, and Terry undertook this aspect considering his greater expertise in the archaeological field. As is his wont, Terry has provided a more thorough introduction that well establishes our starting point, while at the same time systematically setting up a basis for our argument.

Most archaeological discussions of the origins of language focus upon the human paleontology of the late Middle and early Upper Paleolithic, and especially on the differences between the archaic members of the genus *Homo*, including those known as Neanderthals, versus fully modern *Homo sapiens sapiens*. Our perspective also requires looking at the longer evolutionary sequence of the hominid lineages, but for present purposes a brief discussion of the significance of the Upper Paleolithic will be useful. We will defer a view of the longer term until a later chapter. Suffice it to say that general statements about the origins of language in most treatments we have encountered are either incomplete in their grounding or premature in their application of the term "language." This is in part a result of linguistic biases we share across much of academia, as well as specific biases grounded in structural and historical linguistics. Throughout our discussion, we try to separate clearly the idea of language as a "system of pragmatic communication" versus language as a "system for modeling the world based upon experience." We remind our reader that we sometimes use the term "semiosis" to indicate "experience through sign processes." Keep in mind also that sign processes do not necessarily employ "symbols."

With archaic *Homo sapiens*, paleontologists observe that cranial capacity, and possibly topography of the brain (Donald 1991, 101), had reached its present form (Cunliffe 1994, 22). Even the *Homo sapiens neanderthalensis*, with its peculiar skull formation—long, with a low forehead and prominent brow ridge, noticeable prognathism, and an enlarged occipital area (Jurmain, Nelson, and Turnbaugh 1987, 421; Poirier 1977, 252)—still exhibits a sufficiently enlarged neocortex for most to presume the capability for the high cognitive associations that support language and define modern man (Pfeiffer 1982, 41). The brain had, ostensibly, developed its particular physical configuration and the structure extant today. This, then, seems to be a reasonable point at which to place the existence of some sort of language, since the trend toward increasing brain size is presumed to be attendant with developing structures that are now known to house the areas controlling much of language and speech behavior (Donald 1991, 113). However, there is little cultural evidence indicating language capabilities either among Neanderthals or the other early archaic *Homo sapiens* populations (Cunliffe 1994, 36 and 59; Shreeve 1995, 183).

The archaeological record can provide some means for interpreting stages of language development. Each particular era provides the researcher with evidence for innovations that, presumably, must also have been made in conjunction with an increased communicative ability (Aiello and Dunbar 1993, 184; Donald 1991, 122–23; Pfeiffer 1982, 52 and 69). But, at which point is the technology sufficient, or societal data convincing enough, to necessitate the association of language? The argument seems to be most persuasive for the Upper Paleolithic. Here we see a relatively rapid and intense increase in the complexity of the tool assemblage and evidence for social or cooperative action (Cunliffe 1994, 45–53; Donald 1991, 211; Pfeiffer 1982, 13 and 42–52). When these changes are placed in contrast to the very slow developments noted over the previous millions of years, including the era of the Neanderthals, it seems only logical that language use be presumed for the Upper Paleolithic. This is particularly so if language is associated with other forms of higher-level thinking and problem solving (Cunliffe 1994, 58).

What is identified as Upper Paleolithic was for many years assigned exclusively to the Aurignacian "tradition" and tied to modern *Homo sapiens*. This is reasonable because the sites yield major elaboration of stone implements and basic tool forms into much more complex lithic repertoires, including the production of "blades" from prepared cores, complex core reduction routines, use of bone tools and composite tools, the earliest stone figurines, painting with charcoal and ochre, and other decorative or "symbolic" artifacts such as beads (Brantingham, Kuhn, and Kerry 2004: see also Svoboda 2004; Vishnyatsky and Nehoroskey 2004; Meshzeliani, Bar-Yosef, and Belfercohen 2004; Goebel 2004; Kuhn, Stiner, and Güleç 2004 in the same volume). However, the most recent assessments of the emergent Upper Paleolithic in Europe, the Near East, and Eurasia show a complex variability of local and regional patterns, so much so that the well-documented Aurignacian assemblages of Western Europe can no longer be taken as an exclusive baseline for assessing the transition from the Middle Paleolithic (Brantingham, Kuhn, and Kerry 2004, xiii–xiv). Indeed, it is apparent that there are several locally independent late–Middle Paleolithic evolutions of blade industries across much of Western Europe and Eurasia, grounded in either Mousterian (i.e., "Neanderthal") or other archaic human populations. This complicated view began several decades ago with the critique of work by François Bordes that assigned tool "types" and "cultures" for the Mousterian. Analysis by Louis Binford suggested that the Bordes' proposed time-space differences were "functional" and not the results of different cultures (see Wargo 2009). In a slightly different critique of Bordes, Harold Dibble suggested that different "types" of scrapers in the Mousterian were actually stages in the "reduction" of tools through re-use, rather than products of design as specific implements (Dibble 1995). The long-term discussion of these issues has brought some clarification on the technological front, but as more sites involved in the transition to the Upper Paleolithic are studied, it is apparent that the process is not a uniform one in time or space.

What has emerged over the past thirty years of study in the Near East and Western Europe is an understanding that the period from about sixty thousand to thirty-five thousand years ago manifests diverse small populations, not always clearly modern biologically, sometimes in direct competition, sometimes engaging different habitats and resources of a region while living in near proximity, and representing independent blade industries that complement the ultimate expansion of the Aurignacian. The recent work over a wide area expands this picture geographically to western Asia, with somewhat different local manifestations of the transition from subregion to subregion. The potential contributions of the indigenous technological achievements versus adoption of Aurignacian technology remain to be fully elucidated, although it is clear that the balance of influences may involve several regional variations (Brantingham, Kuhn, and Kerry 2004, 242–48).

Adding to this, the general current view is that the physiological distinctions between Archaic *Homo sapiens* and fully modern humans do not represent clear-cut differences in functionality or capacities. Study of the human paleontology of the period is hampered by a lack of skeletal remains in clear association with most of the archaeological manifestations. The importance of very early South African Upper Paleolithic populations to the Eurasian and Near East developments also suffers from a lack of comparable assemblages or evidence of direct continuities. What we do know is that some South African sites show evidences of what archaeologists have called the earliest indications of "symbolism" for *Homo sapiens* at about fifty thousand to seventy thousand years ago (d'Errico et al. 2005). However, human migrations into Australia occurred as early as sixty thousand years ago, before the clear emergence of the Upper Paleolithic elsewhere (Bar-Yosef 2002, 382). This underscores a point that the biological assessment of *Homo sapiens sapiens* versus Archaic humans in other parts of the Old World seems far from settled. What is important for our argument is that the biological forms of the Middle and Upper Paleolithic were all, or perhaps mostly, part of a widespread emergence of modern *Homo sapiens*, and that whether "developed" or "ancestral" or not, they all had similar capacities for the recognition of patterns and the propositional semiosis to follow through relatively complex analytical routines. To what extent such routines were enhanced by symbolic communication remains to be argued, though it is clear that all of the blade industries of the Upper Paleolithic suggest multistage linear processing of information—the potential to "imagine" beyond the immediate circumstances some end product or outcome.

What stone technology suggests about the biological emergence of modern *Homo sapiens*, then, is that the broad development of blade industries and the innovations on stone cores from which they were produced are part of a general process. As Brantingham, Kuhn, and Kerry (2004) have recently expressed the situation, the stone tool developments toward the Upper Paleolithic are neither isolated nor particularly surprising (246):

> Some may agree that a transition to Upper Paleolithic lithic technology was a relatively easy thing to accomplish, although many researchers contend that such "transitional" lithic technologies are simply terminal middle Paleolithic industries, and are therefore of no great relevance to the origins of modern behavior.

We disagree with the qualifying point at the end of this observation, since the emerging complexity of lithic technology over essentially the entire Old World suggests general sign processes that are moving deeper into complex linear (i.e., analytical) cognitive experience. Such elaboration would clearly be a precursor to many of the other elements of Upper Paleolithic culture, even if not augmented through the use of symbolic rhemes (words) or dicents (verbal propositions).

Brantingham, Kuhn, and Kerry (2004) add to the above statement a qualification that is also central to our argument (246): "it is worth considering the possibility that transitions in other domains, such as in the emergence of complex social and symbolic behavior, were far more difficult than those involving lithic technology." True enough, but that does not mean that such elements appear independently of lithic technology developments or the cognitive capacities they signal. Ultimately, all of the manifestations and potential capabilities of the species must be taken as stemming from similar cognitive capacities.

No matter the specifics, what we view as a "transition" from the Middle Paleolithic to the Upper Paleolithic involves some major changes in physiology and behavior. This is firmly shown in the differences between Archaic forms and fully Modern forms in the skeletal evidence we have, even when the remains cannot be said to represent a continuous population. Biologically, the story of modern human dominance over much of the Old World involves many very small groups, widely scattered and undergoing different evolutionary pressures, often pursuing different patterns of subsistence in many kinds of habitats, with a common base gene pool undergoing parallel or more local developments depending upon circumstances, often supplemented by gene-flow and selection across the whole distribution of the genus *Homo*.

SOME PARTICULAR MANIFESTATIONS

Because there has been much more research in Europe and the Near East over a longer period of time, those regions provides the strongest indications of the pattern just noted, with the best examples of demonstrable population differences. In the Levant region of the Near East, studies have identified different ecological orientations for closely proximate populations associated with specific physiologies; while in Spain, remains also show skeletal evidence of association between the Châtelperronian "Upper Paleolithic" technology and a physiologically Neanderthal population (*Homo neanderthalensis* or *Homo sapiens neanderthalensis* in alternative classifications) (Bar-Yosef and Bordes 2010; see also Discamps, Jaubert, and Bachellerie 2011). This population represents the latest continuity of demonstrably Middle Paleolithic people in Europe. Meanwhile, the Aurignacian pattern(s) of Europe proper appear to be the remains of *Homo sapiens sapiens* but do not show consistent technological continuity over the wider Eurasian continent, even among chronologically later remains.

Adding to this complex situation is the presence of substantial examples of cave art dating from about thirty-five thousand to twenty thousand years ago (see Chapter 6, this volume). The time frame could include some Middle Paleolithic populations, but the bulk of the paintings seem firmly associated with Upper Paleolithic people. Cave paintings involve charcoal and ochre applications depicting animals, but including also negative silhouettes of human hands, as well as purely "symbolic" marks. Iconic representations that signal cognitive changes for the genus *Homo* are not seen in many of the earlier archaeological contexts, that is to say for the earliest Archaic members of the genus *Homo*. There are a few tantalizing exceptions coming to light in well-dated cave marks from Spain (Hoffmann, Standish et al. 2018), pushing dated material back to sixty-five thousand years ago. The negative outlines of human hands produced by charcoal blown over the hand on the cave walls also represent the earliest, possibly pre-thirty-five-thousand-year-old activity, suggesting many individual events that some have attributed to initiation rites.

Of all the Upper Paleolithic evidence in the record, cave art has led to the widest range of speculations about human cognition, the emergence of "culture" as we know it, and potentially language. Popular fascination with the animal representations of Chauvet and Lascaux in France, and Altamira in Spain, has stressed the earliest of such paintings as suggesting "language." What we should emphasize at this point (elaborated later) is that the paintings do not represent human figures, tend to be overlapping individual works, and are in what are otherwise difficult or nearly inaccessible locations within the caves. There are no "weapons" or "hunting scenes" in these caves, but the quality of the depictions is so sophisticated in iconicity that the earliest assessments erroneously suggested that they were not of great antiquity.

In effect, Western European cave paintings represent full-blown "iconic realism" without any "simpler" aesthetic foundation. Interestingly, as we will demonstrate in our fuller discussion, the more "abstracted" stick figures of later eras appear simpler, but are indicative of a more selective and analytically engaged thought process. Indeed, analysis and dating demonstrate that cave art generally contrasts with highly abstracted narrative images of humans in the rock art of later periods right up to the present. Our analysis of the full range of paintings from all periods is one of the central elements of our view of language origins, tying the forms and artistic techniques to the shift from a primarily "holistic" mode of human cognition toward a more "analytical" and "sequential" mode of thinking.

The main discussions of the Upper Paleolithic all focus upon the emergence and spread of blade technologies across much of the Old World, coupled with hints of "symbolic" activity, somewhat independently of cave art analyses. Taken together with the information on lithic technology, ornamentation, living sites, community interactions, and shelter construction, the data from cave art may be explained with reference to the development of semiotic capacities of the species, and ultimately to the emergence of the "symbolic argument" in human populations. In other terms, we will present the evidences in later chapters that the emergence of "language" as a modeling system is concurrent with the emergence of the capacity for the *symbolic argument*, which was initiated mainly within the Upper Paleolithic, especially in the later stages of that period, as *Homo sapiens sapiens* came to dominate the Old World.

In brief, the semiotic explanation of the Old World data as we know it today reinforces the idea that both Archaic and Modern populations of the genus *Homo* possessed the capacity to formulate and manipulate novel *symbolic rhemes* (words or visual symbols) and *dicents* (propositions created by associating rhemes) representing iconic and indexical capacities shared widely among the Hominoidea. Additionally, recent research by Genevieve Von Petzinger on non-representational signs that accompany the paintings (see especially 2011, 2017) strongly reinforces these interpretations of symbolic capacities during the late Middle and early Upper Paleolithic. Sharing these foundational symbols (rhemes and dicents) in simple "speech acts" between individuals would have conferred some survival advantages, augmenting the ability to "observe" and "connect" phenomena—in effect, to learn particular tasks symbolically as well as visually. But the ability to construct "models" of incipient behavior in tool making, planning in hunting and gathering, and other social activities requiring manipulation of larger representational sets—essentially narrative sets removed from context—seem not to be in ubiquitous play. Overall, the Paleolithic record suggests expansions of ability shifting emphasis of "experience" from icons and indices, per se, to a richer symbolic stream capable of producing the technological and social embellishments amply manifest in the late Upper Paleolithic, and foundational to all later periods. In our view, we are making a distinction between simple "speech acts" in context, versus habitual symbolling as an overarching approach to the world. Our task is to detail some of the cognitive systems and capacities that enabled such a transition, but in order to do that we must now review a wide range of other studies that have aided in our particular assessment of the "problem" of language origins in a heterogeneous and widely spread population of co-founders.

WORKS CITED

Aiello, L. C., and R. I. M. Dunbar. 1993. "Neocortex Size, Group Size, and the Evolution of Language." *Current Anthropology* 34: 2.

Bar-Yosef, Ofer. 2002. "The Upper Paleolithic Revolution." *Annual Review of Anthropology* 31: 363–93.

Bar-Yosef, Ofer, and Jean-Gyillaume Bordes. 2010. "Who Were the Makers of the Châtelperronian Culture?" *Journal of Human Evolution* 59 (5): 586–93.

Brantingham, P. Jeffrey, Steven L. Kuhn, and Kristopher W. Kerry, ed. 2004. *The Early Upper Paleolithic beyond Western Europe*. Berkeley: University of California Press.

Cunliffe, B. 1994. *The Oxford Illustrated Prehistory of Europe*. Oxford: Oxford University Press.

Dibble, H. L. 1995. "Middle Paleolithic Scraper Reduction: Background, Clarification, and Review of the Evidence to Date." *Journal of Archaeological Method and Theory* 2: 299–368.

Discamps, Emmanuel, Jacques Jaubert, and François Bachellerie. 2011. "Human Choices and Environmental Constraints: Deciphering the Variability of Large Game Procurement from Mousterian to Aurignacian Times (MIS 5-3) in Southwestern France. *Quaternary Science Reviews* 30 (19–20): 2755–75. https://www.sciencedirect.com/science/article/abs/pii/S0277379111001818?via%3Dihub.

Donald, Merlin. 1991. *Origins of the Modern Mind: Three Stages in the Evolution of Culture and Cognition*. Cambridge, MA: Harvard University Press.

d'Errico, Francesco, et al. 2005. "*Nassarius kraussianus* Shell Beads from Blombos Cave: Evidence for Symbolic Behaviour in the Middle Stone Age." *Journal of Human Evolution* 48: 3–24.

Goebel, T. 2004. "The Early Upper Paleolithic of Siberia." In *The Early Upper Paleolithic beyond Western Europe*, edited by P. Jeffrey Brantingham, Steven L. Kuhn, and Kristopher W. Kerry, 162–95. Berkeley: University of California Press.

Hoffmann, D. L., C. D. Standish, et al. 2018. "U-Th Dating of Carbonate Crusts Reveals Neandertal Origin of Iberian Cave Art." *Science* 359 (6378): 912–15.

Jurmain, R., H. Nelson, and W. A. Turnbaugh. 1987. *Understanding Physical Anthropology and Archeology*. New York: West Publishing Company.

Kuhn, S. L., M. C. Stiner, and E. Güleç. 2004. "New Perspectives on the Initial Upper Paleolithic: The View from Üçağızlı Cave, Turkey." In *The Early Upper Paleolithic beyond Western Europe*, edited by P. Jeffrey Brantingham, Steven L. Kuhn, and Kristopher W. Kerry, 113–28. Berkeley: University of California Press.

Poirier, F. E. 1977. *Fossil Evidence: The Human Evolutionary Journey*. St. Louis: C. V. Mosby Company.

Pfeiffer, John E. 1982. *The Creative Explosion: An Inquiry into the Origin of Art and Religion*. New York: Harper and Row.

Shreeve, J. 1995. *The Neanderthal Enigma: The Mystery of Modern Human Origins*. New York: William Morrow and Company, Inc.

Vishnyatsky, L. B., and P. E. Nehoroshev. 2004. "The Beginning of the Upper Paleolithic on the Russian Plain." In *The Early Upper Paleolithic beyond Western Europe*, edited by P. Jeffrey Brantingham, Steven L. Kuhn, and Kristopher W. Kerry, 80–96. Berkeley: University of California Press.

Von Petzinger, Genevieve, and April Nowell. 2011. "A Question of Style: Reconsidering the Stylistic Approach to Dating Paleolithic Parietal Art in France." *Antiquity* 85: 1165–83.

——— 2017. *The First Signs: Unlocking the Mysteries of the World's Oldest Symbols*. New York: Simon & Schuster.

Wargo, Melissa Canady. 2009. "The Bordes-Binford Debate: Transatlantic Interpretive Traditions in Paleolithic Archaeology." Doctoral dissertation: The University of Texas at Arlington. https://uta-ir.tdl.org/uta-ir/bitstream/handle/10106/1766/Wargo_uta_2502D_10351.pdf?sequence=1.

Chapter Four

Encountering Autism

Karen's Story: Once assured that my memories about the archaeological record for the Upper Paleolithic were still in keeping with my initial ideas on the evolutionary sequence, I felt I was ready to begin researching in earnest the syndrome of autism. My first step, of course, was a return to the case presented in the documentary, which initially provoked those ideas. I obtained a copy of Lorna Selfe's published volume on Nadia (Selfe 1977). The book is well illustrated with example after example of Nadia's amazing drawings, confirming my memory of what I had seen on television. Nadia's sketches of animals were indeed impressive, even more so when they were presented alongside more typical childhood drawings. The volume presented a thorough investigation of Nadia's history, talents, and aptitudes and proved to be a solid foundational step for my studies.

The parents of Nadia Chomyn sought out the help of the Child Development Research Unit at the University of Nottingham, when at the age of six Nadia had not progressed in her language skills beyond her initial vocabulary of a few words learned in her first year. Previously, this organization had conducted a broad study of childhood art involving analysis of twenty-four thousand "pictures of mummy" that had been submitted for a local art competition. They felt they had a thorough grounding and understanding of childhood creativity. But, when Nadia's mother produced a sampling of drawings produced beginning at the age of three, these notions were to be challenged. Lorna Selfe was one of the psychologists who participated in the initial session with Nadia, and, once Nadia's drawing capabilities were witnessed firsthand a few days later, Selfe resolved to embark on an extensive case study (Selfe 1977, 1–2).

Selfe found that Nadia's general behavior was of a sluggish detached demeanor exhibiting poor muscle tone and coordination. Until, that is, she was provided with some paper and a felt-tip pen. She preferred the precision of this instrument over the broad strokes of crayons or brushes. When the mood was right, Nadia would produce quick, but exceptional, sketches (Selfe 1977, 8–13): "She generally drew swiftly and deftly, becoming animated—in marked contrast to her normal lethargic behavior. . . . This usually gave her great pleasure and after surveying intently what she had drawn she often smiled, babbled and shook her hands and knees in glee." These sketches evidently provided Nadia with a delightful sense of accomplishment.

Based on the received view in psychology on childhood development, child drawing can be a measure of cognitive development, indicating conceptualization of surroundings, perceptual reality, represented as symbols, as well as word acquisition. Features of realism, such as perspective, foreshortening and proportion, then, are considered indications of maturity and for the most part some form of learned training. But Nadia's drawings exhibited all these aspects of the mature artist (Selfe 1977, 98).

Nadia's drawings appear to be drawn from life, and she did have some firsthand experience with the animals she drew from trips to parks and the local zoo. But it seems her primary inspiration came from the simplistic outline drawings of animals in her children's books. Her drawings could be quite accurate reproductions of her favorites, though these were always produced from memory. In addition, however, she could also adjust angles of representation, sometimes even reversing the image, and add movement, emotion, and vitality to the original staid depictions. It seems that she was making use of her three-dimensional experience to elaborate and expand on the original image. Nadia would also sometimes place one or more images over another on a single sheet of paper during a drawing session, which seems to indicate that the activity of drawing, not the final product, is what was important to her. In contrast, more typical children, who have acquired considerable linguistic capabilities by the time their eye-hand coordination allows for experimentation in depiction, have already begun the process of schematicizing their visual world. Selfe quotes Karl Buhler from his study on childhood development from 1930 (Buhler in Selfe 1977, 104), "Drawings are graphic accounts of essentially verbal processes. As an essentially verbal education gains control, the child abandons his graphic efforts and relies almost entirely on words. Language has first spoilt drawing and then swallowed it up completely." For Selfe (1977), Nadia's drawing activity seemed to illustrate how the conceptualization process may progress without the dominance of the linguistic mode.

> Nadia showed us that it is possible to draw without conceptualization, when conceptualization is narrowly conceived as being solely linguistic in nature. However, conceptualization can also be in terms of perceptual and spatial im-

ages, and Nadia showed us that psychologists . . . have underestimated the importance and richness of perceptual and spatial conceptualization. (127)

In her concluding remarks, Selfe (1977, 127) also went on to note that language may become a "shorthand for reality" that supersedes mental imagery during childhood development. This notion suggests an efficiency to the linguistic mode, which became significant to our development of arguments on the evolutionary sequence of linguistic thought, and it will come up again later in this volume.

In general, Selfe's study of Nadia's works consisted of an attempt to reconcile the drawings with the standard modes of analysis for normative childhood drawing. In each case, of course, the sketches far surpassed the expectations of other children of a comparable age. And in the end, Selfe (1977, 128) surmised that Nadia's "ability was so outside the range of normal activity that comparisons on the basis of such normative and qualitative adjectives are misplaced." For me, Nadia's case signals a defect in the standard modes of study in psychology and education, and in the social sciences in general. Standardized statistical models can be very effective, efficient, and powerful means of assessing behavior. However, if these systems are not designed to show flexibility in the face of aberrant data, then there is a real danger of becoming virtually blind to the full range of variability that one knows must be more relevant to actual reality. Being open to the variations of thought and perception allows us to expand the realm of possibility and move out of the tyranny of the dominant mode in the self, as well as in society, a lesson that seems common to many poets, philosophers, and gurus over the ages.

In December of 2015, *The Guardian* issued an online obituary by Lorne Selfe announcing Nadia Chomyn's death in October, after a short illness at the age of forty-eight. Selfe points out that Nadia's history may provide an illustration of the notion of linguistic predominance in cognition by noting that as she developed skills in verbal communication through extensive training, her drawing sessions dwindled, as did her virtuosity in realism. She also pointed out that Nadia's case remains today a singular and exceptional example of artistic ability in a child (2015): "When her work was first published, no similar case had been reported, although a few retrospective studies of adults with savant skills existed. Other autistic artists and savants have been identified and studied in the intervening years, but none have shown such prodigious ability at such an early age."

> *My extended assessment of the case study on Nadia had further convinced me that I was looking in the right direction in stressing the visual capabilities of the autistic population. It was time, then, to gain a more complete knowledge of the syndrome. Unfortunately, my forays into the academic record on autism*

proved very frustrating and quite unfruitful. The psychology research on autism in the early 1990s was scant, as the syndrome had only in recent decades been determined to be a problem distinct from schizophrenia. Also, diagnosis was still quite rare, with a rate of 1 person in 2500 (in the 1980s the rate was listed as 1 in 10,000) (Autism Science Foundation 2020). The early publications of research into the syndrome did little more than describe the behavioral difficulties and deficiencies of the young children with autism and present suppositions about the nature of the autistic mind, some of which I later found to be misguided. I found only guesswork about a population of troubled youngsters who were quite incapable of reporting their own experience.

Although frustrated at the paltry information provided by the sources encountered at the university library, I knew from the interest shown from the documentary on Nadia that there had to be other materials out there. I decided to check out works in the popular press at a local bookstore. Here I hit pay dirt: books whose authors were autistic themselves. I could gather firsthand information on cognitive development and thought processes of the autistic mind.

AUTISTIC BIOGRAPHY AND AUTOBIOGRAPHY

Works by authors with autism (Williams 1992, 1994; Sacks 1995; Prince-Hughes 2001, 2004; Grandin and Scariano 1986; Grandin 1996; Grandin and Johnson 2005; Martin 1994) bring to light several important points about autism in general. These works suggest to us that autism results from a developmental disorder related to a difficulty in the processing of novel stimuli. This leads children to be inundated with sensory inputs with no mechanisms for dealing with them. There are no filters, and no automatic process of learning a classification system. Recognizing this aspect of their experience helps one begin to understand what autistic children are up against, and it provides the basis for recognizing the anguish behind the behavioral difficulties so prevalent in the reports of autistic case studies. The autistic child must develop his or her own *conscious* methods of dealing with sensory input. This begins to explain the repetitive behavioral repertoire and the intense need for order and sameness in their surroundings, and their attempts to keep novel experience to a minimum.

Such coping mechanisms must be developed during the time when normal children are soaking up their surroundings and using this input for the development of logical thinking and communication. In turn, this leads to a vast array of differences within the autistic community. The variations in the extent of the neural disorder, coupled with the individual home and training scenarios, lead to a marked level of difference with each case. There exist many more-complete discussions of the typical developmental sequence for children, but we must note that the autistic child is too preoccupied with generalized sensory input to be able to concentrate on or participate in standard social or linguistic cueing at important stages of brain development. The difficulty is especially prominent during early stages of synaptogenesis and myelination, processes that will be discussed more fully in Chapter 10. For the autistic child, learning to communicate must become a purely conscious experience in a later time frame, not the automatic aspect of the standard developmental process.

The point to be made here is that standard studies of childhood development belie the extent to which people with autism are linguistically challenged. The children with autism studied in the generalized research were considered to be severely deficient in language capability. Instead, you find that speech communication is simply not present *at the same time* during development as in the normative population. If there are books written by those with autism, then obviously the language deficits of early developmental stages may, though not always, be overcome in later years. For many, language development may only be delayed, though for some there are too many other attendant problems to make language a possibility. Some level of language is of course a capability for these children, since all of us are modern *Homo sapiens*. But, where many of us take on some skills as a learned and conscious endeavor in later childhood (tying shoe laces, whistling, blowing bubbles, reading a clock, literacy), the autistic person must make an effort to learn sentence structure, conversational cues, and facial and gestural signs. Hence, eventually, individuals with autism can report on their childhood and inform the psychological community in rare ways, particularly when one finds that prodigious memory capabilities are also a part of the autistic syndrome in some individuals. Also, many of these people have now become well known to the population at large and are definitely part of the online world accessed by others learning to deal with their autism, as well as by parents learning to deal with autistic children.

All in all, what can be learned through the self-reports of these authors is a mode of thought that elucidates the complexities of human cognition, helping to separate out various forms of thought with an eye toward understanding human diversity and how human cognition changed over time in the evolutionary process.

Donna Williams' account of her childhood and early adult years in *Nobody Nowhere* (1992) became a bestseller and hence was available in our local bookstore. Her story of early life was amazing to say the least. For the first time one could get a glimpse into the strange world of a childhood beset by external stimuli. Bernard Rimland noted in his foreword (Williams 1992, x):

> Much of what Donna Williams has written about the experience of autism was already familiar to me—at an intellectual level. But *Nobody Nowhere* provides a

heretofore unavailable—and alarming—highly subjective appreciation of what it is like to be autistic.

Williams' survival is even more amazing when you realize that her efforts to make sense of the external world were almost entirely solitary and without any notion of the cause of her disconnect (she never heard the term "autistic" until her college years). Her accounts of her personal and lonely journey to finding coping mechanisms were fascinating, yet heartbreaking. And although her record of her means of dealing with the confusion in encountering "the world" in childhood are exemplary, I find her direct and candid chronicle of her journey into adulthood to be the most amazing aspect of her story. She provides the most vivid and honest tale of self-actualization one might ever hope to encounter.

It seems Williams' mode of encountering the world in general was through the experience of minutia, from the "bright spots" of her hypersensitive visual world to the favorite "tinkles" she noted and enjoyed in her world of sounds. Hers was a fragmented world of perceptions that were not easily placed into a logical progression that would provide meaning or understanding. Her earliest attempts at conversation were the echolalic phrases she would hear and remember, but not understand their meaning or their appropriate use in social situations. And though she did not discern in a conscious way the patterning of numbers and sounds, she had an inherent understanding of mathematics and music. Her troubles in math classes did not come from her inability to provide a correct answer, but from an education system that required students to "show their work" to demonstrate how the answer was derived (1992, 120). In music, she had a natural ability but could not fathom the step-by-step instruction required in music classes. The following excerpt is a good representation of how Williams related to her perceptual world and how she tells her story (1992, 74):

> My mother has recently rented a piano, and I loved the sound of anything that tinkled, and had since I was very small. I would string safety pins together and, when I wasn't chewing on them, would tinkle them in my ear. Similarly I loved the sound of metal striking metal, and my two most favorite objects were a piece of cut crystal and a tuning fork, which I carried with me for years. When all else failed, music could always make me feel.
>
> I believe that I had always played music, even before I ever had the use of an instrument. I would create tunes in my head, and my fingers would play the intervals.
>
> My mother also had a passion for classical music and had decided to teach herself to play.
>
> As soon as I had noticed it, I was at the piano in a flash. Within a few minutes I was tapping out tunes, playing them quite fluently. It had occurred to me at

the time that this is what I had been doing with my fingers when I had heard music in my head.

Williams' early adult life was beset by an inability to function in normal social situations, but she persevered and even eventually obtained degrees in linguistics, sociology, and education. It was through her studies that she sought to understand her differences with others, finally confirming her self-diagnosis in her early twenties. She also recognized the deficiencies in the academic record on autism, which brought her to write and publish her story. She published four autobiographies and served as an international speaker and consultant on the autistic spectrum.

Donna Williams considered herself primarily an artist and musician; her creative acts working to help elicit meaning. As she noted on her webpage (2017):

> My mind was like a mosaic, my conscious thoughts intangible until I experienced them after they'd been expressed—usually through arts. I am still always surprised, have a great trust of unknown knowing, and have come to allow my preconscious mind to unravel and surprise me. I'm a systematician but otherwise I'm a doer. Only through doing can I realise what my intangible thoughts may have been.

Williams released two albums of her musical compositions and produced a number of paintings and sculpture works. Although she suffered throughout her life with a range of other physiological difficulties, such as Primary Immune Deficiencies, Hypoventilation Syndrome, and Ehlers-Danlos syndrome, she always persevered, even through a battle with breast cancer that finally took her life in 2017 at the age of fifty-three. We recommend a browse through her webpage to get a glimpse of her life story and artworks and to read her stalwart and inspiring message about overcoming hardship.

> *Encouraged by the insights provided by reading Donna Williams' story, I ventured again into works in popular culture to continue my study of the autism spectrum. This time I encountered the work of a noted neurologist, Oliver Sacks, entitled* An Anthropologist on Mars *(1995). Sacks, through his publications written for the general population, was bringing much of the world of psychological research into the public realm. And this particular book provided a series of chapters on the various psychological phenomena, including two chapters on people with autism, Stephen Wiltshire and Temple Grandin. Both of these people have gone on to be well known for their achievements, but his book served to introduce them both to a wider reading public.*

Stephen Wiltshire, like Nadia, found his primary means of expression in the visual arts. And like Nadia, he could produce amazing representations without training and completely from memory. But where Nadia was mostly interested in the depiction of animals, Steven loved to render architectural subjects. At the time of Sacks' first introduction to Stephen, he was only fourteen years old but already well known for his artistic feats. He was fortunate to be surrounded with supportive family, friends, and teachers, who were anxious to share his gift with others; a book of his sketches of various sites around London drawn at the age of ten had been published (Wiltshire 1987).

Selfe's record on Nadia's artwork stressed her ability to render her animals with life and movement. Sacks notes that Stephen's works were primarily feats of memory. Stephen is able to record in minute and accurate detail what he has seen. As Sacks notes (1995, 200), "It seemed to make no difference whether he drew from life or from the images in his memory. He needed no aide-mémorie, no sketches or notes—a single sidelong glance, lasting only a few seconds, was enough." Stephen's memory of visual input was almost photographic in nature, what psychologists now refer to as eidetic memory. However, Sacks noted, significantly, that Stephen's drawings were not mechanically accurate, but were imbued with subtle changes that personalized his perception of the scene (206). Stephen's teachers stressed that his skills were not *taught*, but that he seemed to have an innate sense of techniques (199). When asked, he is also capable of reproducing other's artworks. For instance, he reproduced a Matisse portrait several times over one afternoon, each time making a drawing that was not precisely accurate but which evoked the artist's style (213).

In addition, Wiltshire's perceptual memory skills did not center on only the visual (Sacks 1995, 200):

> He was very good at mime, even before he was able to speak. He had an excellent memory for songs and would reproduce these with great accuracy. He could copy any movement to perfection. Thus Stephen, at eight, showed an ability to grasp, retain, and reproduce the most complex visual, auditory, motor, and verbal patterns, apparently irrespective of their context, significance, or meaning.

Therefore, when Stephen decided to take music lessons several years later, he exhibited a similar natural understanding of the medium. His instructor noted that he seemed to possess an innate sense of musical intervals (thirds, fifths, sevenths) and at the same time was capable of the improvisational aspects of jazz, complete with personal feeling and creativity (239). Over the years, Stephen has continued to impress others with his artistic skills. As an adult, he is an established professional artist. Examples of his works are available on the internet (2005).

At the time of Sacks' interview with Temple Grandin for his second chapter on autism in his 1995 book, she was already an established expert in her field in animal husbandry, and she has since become a prime mover in educating others on the nature of autism. There was even a movie about her life made in 2010 (*Temple Grandin*, Mick Jackson, dir.). Unlike Donna Williams' childhood, Temple Grandin had great support from her mother, who worked tirelessly to provide her with educational opportunities, going against the standard treatment of the time of institutionalization for children with autism. Grandin's books are an excellent guide to finding one's personal means for navigating the world of normalcy. In fact, Sacks' title for his book comes from Grandin's own description of her studies into normal human interaction; she feels it is like being "an anthropologist on Mars" (1995, 259).

I have continued to keep abreast of the writings of autistic subjects but have found that Grandin's insightful record of her own life served to define several standard aspects of autism that are significant in helping to elucidate the nature of the development of language in humans. My next step, then, given a chapter of its own here, was to delve into Grandin's own works, which include a series of books written expressly to help others learn to cope with their differences.

WORKS CITED

Autism Science Foundation. 2020. "What Is Autism." http://autismsciencefoundation.org/what-is-autism/how-common-is-autism/.

Grandin, Temple, and Margaret M. Scariano. 1986. *Emergence: Labeled Autistic*. Novato, CA: Arena Press.

Grandin, Temple. 1996. *Thinking in Pictures and Other Reports from My Life with Autism*. New York: Doubleday.

Grandin, Temple, and Catherine Johnson. 2005. *Animals in Translation: Using the Mysteries of Autism to Decode Animal Behavior*. New York: Harcourt.

Martin, Russell. 1994. *Out of Silence: An Autistic Boy's Journey into Language and Communication*. New York: Penguin Books.

Prince-Hughes, Dawn. 2001. *Gorillas among Us: A Primate Ethnographer's Book of Days*. Tucson: University of Arizona Press.

———. 2004. *Songs of the Gorilla Nation: My Journey through Autism*. New York: Harmony Books.

Sacks, Oliver W. 1995. *An Anthropologist on Mars*. New York: Vintage Books.

Selfe, Lorna. 1977. *Nadia: A Case of Extraordinary Drawing Ability in an Autistic Child*. London: Academic Press.

———. 2015. "Nadia Chomyn Obituary." *The Guardian*, December 9. https://www.theguardian.com/artanddesign/2015/dec/09/nadia-chomyn.

Williams, Donna. 1992. *Nobody Nowhere*. New York: Avon Books.

———. 1994. *Somebody Somewhere: Breaking Free from the World of Autism*. New York: Random House.
———. 2017. http://www.donnawilliams.net/.
Wiltshire, Stephen. 1987. *Drawings, Stephen Wiltshire*. Foreword by Lorraine Cole. London: J. M. Dent and Sons, Ltd.
———. 2005. http://www.stephenwilshire.co.uk/index.php.

Chapter Five

Cognitive Styles

Karen's Story: Temple Grandin's life story presents an inspiring example of all that can be accomplished despite the challenges of autism. She earned multiple university degrees: a bachelor's degree in psychology from Franklin Pierce College, a master's in animal science from Arizona State University, and a doctorate in animal science from University of Illinois. She is currently a professor at Colorado State University. In addition, she has had a spectacular career in the meat-production industry, having created revolutionary designs for animal-handling systems and slaughterhouses.

On top of these impressive personal successes, Grandin has taken on a full second career in writing and lecturing, working toward a better understanding of and methods for coping with autism. The challenges for those with autism are myriad and extensive, from rampant allergies to the constant state of alarm that comes from overstimulation. The body is overtaxed by the autonomic fight-or-flight reaction that keeps one in almost constant adrenaline-induced panic mode. Medications are necessary to keep this in check, as well as strategies for long-term management of the medication dosage. And, of course, there are the all-encompassing pressures of dealing with society in general.

Grandin's works provide thorough and valuable guidance for developing coping strategies, but for my purposes I focused on her contributions to understanding the syndrome and the implications behind the distinctive cognitive processes of autism. It was clear from my general reading that there is an underlying basic variance in the world that is experienced in autism. Moreover, this difference centers around a set of inherent talents and capabilities that may shed light on the enigmas of the Upper Paleolithic. Grandin's works go beyond a simple record of her story, as she generalizes about cognition from her own experiences. Therefore, I focused on her illustrations of visual thinking in autism.

Temple Grandin's primary theme in her 1995 volume *Thinking in Pictures* is the need for a general acceptance that there are very basic differences in thought process across human populations, and that there is an erroneous assumption in the scientific and academic arenas that language is necessary for thought. Her first sentence states (19), "I think in pictures." The fact that this style of cognition was in opposition to most others around her didn't become clear until her college years, when she read a scientific article that claimed the development of tool use in prehistoric humans must follow the development of language. This was an absurd notion to one who creates and conceives her designs purely through visualization (27, 159). Moreover, this visualized thought, in Grandin's case, is phenomenal. Her mental realm is not filled with simple static screenshots of past events, but with dynamic three-dimensional visual arrays that can be mentally manipulated in order to view her world from various angles. She notes that the images are comparable to a computer graphics program and uses this ability in her work designing equipment and facilities for the livestock industry (21):

> When I do an equipment simulation in my imagination or work on an engineering problem, it is like seeing it on a videotape in my mind. I can view it from any angle, placing myself above or below the equipment and rotating it at the same time. I don't need a fancy graphics program that can produce three-dimensional design simulations. I can do it better and faster in my head.

In addition, these mental simulations improve over time with experience, as she builds her "library" of each element used in her work: gates, fences, latches, ramps, chutes, and so on. Her visualization skills also provide her with the capability to draw the necessary design plans without any formal training in drafting (106).

It is not only the concrete visual world that is built up in Grandin's mental repertoire. In order to understand language, she found that she had to translate what she read or heard in conversation into some sort of concrete visual form, usually through association (25), in order to gain meaning. For example, Grandin notes (30):

> Spatial words such as "over" and "under" had no meaning for me until I had a visual image to fix them in my memory. Even now, when I hear the word "under" by itself, I automatically picture myself getting under the cafeteria tables at school during an air-raid drill. . . . The first memory that any single word triggers is almost always a childhood memory.

She has observed that for the visual thinker these associations can link to an endless succession of memories. Her personal example of the continuing links for the word "under" bring up first, submarines, then the Beatles song *Yellow Submarine*, then people boarding the ship in the song, and next the gangway of a ship she had seen in Austria, and so on. She has learned to quiet this tendency to get lost in association, but she has surmised that often others with autism get caught up in these reveries and find it difficult to switch gears on their own (25). Also, Grandin recognizes that her understanding of grammatical structure is limited. As a child, she had to learn to use certain parts of speech such as articles and prepositions through rote memorization, with no visual component, mimicking the speech patterns of her parents. She states (31), "To this day certain verb conjugations, such as 'to be,' are absolutely meaningless to me."

Grandin's *Thinking in Pictures* (1995) provides an excellent catalogue of many aspects of behavior and physiology that occur in the wide spectrum of autistic traits. Her perspective is enhanced by her considerable personal experience with others in autism as well as a prodigious study of the literature on the subject. But, she constantly reiterates the idea that each individual is unique, varying from biological indicators, such as food allergies, to environmental fluctuations of home and school. She stresses that no one set of coping mechanisms can be adequate for all. The information she provides is an excellent resource for those seeking to understand the phenomenon and learn to adapt in what can be a bewildering external world.

For me, however, her work is significant by her description of visual thinking as an element of autism that she deems widespread and, most importantly, not exclusive to that community. Working as she does in a visually creative realm, she has encountered many who also think in pictures. She also surmises that the exceptional creativity of past figures, such as Einstein (182) or Tesla (26), probably have this style of cognition in common. She notes that capabilities of the memory savants that appear in the academic studies, such as A. R. Luria's *Mind of the Mnemonist* (26, see also Luria 1987) or in popular culture, such as with the movie *Rain Man* (31, see also Levinson 1988), as well as the more general capability for skills like jigsaw puzzling, all probably derive from this cognitive mode. As she notes (27), "Some other people think in vividly detailed pictures, but most think in a combination of words and vague, generalized pictures."

Even within the realm of visual thinking, there are variations in capabilities. Grandin surmises that the savants use a very static though complete visual record of what they see to recall the requested data. For Grandin, visualizations are fluid and able to be manipulated, making the creation of her designs possible. She also notes that these visualizations are not rigid, so that when she has made a mental adjustment to a particular construction design, the original vision of the facility is replaced to her memory (158).

As an illustration of the extent to which visual thinking can be relevant to the savant experience, we can look to yet another autobiographic source, *Born on a Blue Day: Inside the Extraordinary Mind of an Autistic Savant*, by Daniel Tammet (2007). Tammet is considered a math savant and was first brought into notice in 2004 by his public recitation of pi out to 22,514 digits. The event was organized by Tammet as part of a fundraising effort for the United Kingdom's National Society for Epilepsy (174). When describing his techniques for memorization in preparation for the event, Tammet provides a splendid and vivid account of his mental imagery with regard to his world of numbers. He demonstrates the extent to which even mathematics can be linked inextricably to the visual and other perceptual realms (177–78):

> When I look at a sequence of numbers, my head begins to fill with colors, shapes, and textures that knit together spontaneously to form a visual landscape. These are always very beautiful to me; as a child I often spent hours at a time exploring numerical landscapes in my mind. To recall each digit, I simply retrace the different shapes and textures in my head and read the numbers out of them.
>
> Very long numbers, such as pi, I break the digits down into smaller segments. The size of each segment varies, depending on what the digits are. For example, if a number is very bright in my head and the next one very dark, I would visualize them separately, whereas a smooth number followed by another smooth number would be remembered together. As the sequence of digits grows, my numerical landscapes become more complex and layered, until—as with pi—they become like an entire country in my mind, composed of numbers.

Tammet's memorization project for pi became a recall of a flow of visual and other perceptual data reminiscent of Grandin's visual arrays formed in her design processes.

In *Thinking in Pictures* (1995) Grandin also notes that a general weakness in understanding social conventions occurs with visual thinkers. For her the appropriate behavior in social situations had to be learned by rote. She had no inherent understanding of the emotions and motivations behind interactions with others, finding that she was simply an observer rather than a participant (132). For most people, the rules of social interaction come quite naturally without conscious effort, while for those with autism these skills must be obtained systematically, learned like lessons in school (134).

We see an important link between challenges in language and social interaction for the visual thinker, in that both of these skills are obtained by most people early in childhood as part of the developmental process. This brings to the fore the realization that language, as conversation, is an immanently social behavior. Learning language alongside social cuing then becomes central to understanding the differentiations between cognitive styles.

In Sacks' chapter on Grandin, another defining characteristic of the visual thinker is stressed when he recounts the very first interaction with her, a phone conversation where he asked for driving directions from the airport to her office (1995, 255). As she proceeded to provide very precise information on the route, he interrupted at one point to ask for clarification. Grandin proceeded to start the directions again from the beginning. For her, the set of directions was a complete piece of information and was not to be subdivided. Like the visual or audio memories of the savant, the mental realm is composed of distinct wholes. While at the same time, there can be an inherent understanding of musical or mathematical or aesthetic visual relations, *a la* Nadia or Stephen Wiltshire. Possibly, the capability for a heightened interaction with the perceptual world enhances the awareness of the organizing relations within those perceptions in the long run.

Aside from the significance of Grandin's notions about visual thinking in humans, her most important point for my purposes lies in her conviction that visual thinking is the dominant cognitive mode for other animals. Again, she reacts to those in the scientific community who, because they have defined thought in terms of language use, question whether animals can think. She notes that such people are most likely highly verbal with poor visualization skills (1995, 159). She states (1995, 160), "Since I have pictures in my imagination, I assume that animals have similar pictures. Differences between language-based thought and picture-based thoughts may explain why artists and accountants fail to understand each other. They are like apples and oranges."

Grandin feels she is on common cognitive ground with other animals and, on that basis, when observing them she feels less like an outside observer than she does in many of her human interactions. She devoted several chapters of *Thinking in Pictures* (1995*)* to discussing animal behavior and provides many examples of how her successful designs in husbandry come from her autistic sensibilities. She develops her designs by understanding motivations in her subject animals, such as fear (hypervigilant senses) (145), the need for routine (147), and reactions to discomfort (153). She has used these sensibilities to successfully alter the entire industry of animal husbandry. Her accomplishments are astounding and stem from her unique connection with other species. As she states, "I still don't easily recognize subtle social cues for trouble, though I can tell a mile away if an animal is in trouble" (109). Grandin continued her comparisons between autism and animal intelligence in an entire volume published in 2005, *Animals in Translation*, which provides significant insights on understanding animal behavior (Grandin and Johnson 2005).

Grandin is not alone in recognizing the connections with other species. Dawn Prince-Hughes (2001, 2004), in her studies with gorillas and other ape species, began to make her first real inroads into dealing with the social difficulties of Asperger's through her immediate feeling of connection with her subject animals. As a result, she was also able to better inform others on the worldview of another species. She has written a number of volumes on the subject, most notably, *Songs of the Gorilla Nation: My Journey through Autism* (2004).

It is important to reiterate at this point that the world of visual thinking is not confined to autism or other species. Although the autistic population may serve to represent an extreme of the type, the visual thinker is not entirely absent in the rest of the human population. The heightened visual mode evident in autism simply helps make this natural mode of thought more apparent within others. This point was made clear through Karen's work with her colleagues in a university art department. It was made only too evident by the limitations in dealing with the world of words so prevalent in the other areas of the university, and conversely the difficulty of the other departments in comprehending the methods and modes of the artists. Often times Karen also felt particularly at a loss while trying to delve into the world of images. The question, then, is how is the world of words different?

There is an established distinction made in psychology that describes these visual and word avenues of thought as *holistic* and *analytic*. As Oliver Sacks recognized in his interview with Temple Grandin, her memories were in sets of very specific time frames held in very complete detail, but also definitely separated as distinct from other memories. Such collection of data through sets of wholes is a defining aspect of the holistic mind, but the importance here is that the wholes are presented in finer detail than in analytic thinking.

Analytic thought is often also referred to as sequential thinking and hence describes the most prevalent aspect of this type of cognition, that the present is seen through a series of past and potentially future events, one thing following another. As we have mentioned before causal relations are usually inferred, providing the problem-solving aspect that makes this mode of thought necessary to some extent in all species, in operations of iconic and indexical, rhematic and dicent, sinsigns and legisigns. But, where holistic representations are relatively complete, analytic ones are not. Elements of the past are gleaned for the most important aspects of an event, so that only what is considered relevant is placed in memory. The world of sensation is *abstracted* to only essential details, and the parts are then arranged into relevant connections. "This" follows "that" and a narrative unfolds. "This" follows "that" and a sentence unfolds. Most elements of human culture are devices of sequential thought: speech communication, stories, even our games. They are all structured, devised into some kind of order, and manipulated, moving from underlying rhemes and propositions to symbolic propositions and arguments. When linguists search for universals in grammatical structure, they miss the relevance that it is the process of structuring symbols that is universal, not any particular grammar construction or universal underlying experience. This abstraction and ordering of experience in general is a powerful and efficient tool. The importance of this aspect of analytical thought for the evolution of language cannot be overestimated.

For the moment, we should stress the tendency for those who possess dominant "high holistic" or "high analytic" processing (distinctions to be discussed in detail in Chapter 7) to be basically blind to each other's thought processes. Those with an analytical mind organize perceptual surroundings in a way that can be confusing to the highly visual thinker, just as the ability to draw or memorize or compute numbers is daunting to the mainly sequential thinker. The innate ability of the more analytically leaning child to discern complete grammars from the sound stream they hear as toddlers, as well as their ability to learn to negotiate social interaction from subtle cues of the behavior around them, is considered astonishing to the highly visual thinker. Those with high-level holistic capabilities are dubbed "savants," while the normal capabilities for language and social interaction are considered to be equally confusing and awe inspiring to the holistic mind. In effect, most people are what might be called "linguistic savants." In fact, the relationship between holistic and analytic thinking within individuals is much more complex than we are stating at this point—these are not all-or-nothing capacities, and that point will require elaboration in later chapters.

At this juncture in our discussion, we would like to note how these cognitive distinctions can inform research in any number of areas. As an example, we would like to mention the research by Beate Hermelin on the savant syndrome that is summarized in her volume, *Bright Splinters of the Mind: A Personal Story of Research with Autistic Savants* (2001). We found that the research methods involved in this work primarily sought analytical strategies within what must be holistic forms of thought. We also found it limiting to make the distinctions between those with "talents" in the arts, math, or music and those exhibiting skills assessed by the *intelligence* measure of IQ tests, especially as it is noted within the volume that the test was designed by Alfred Binet to seek out those aspects of thought most useful in predicting success in the academic realm (33–34). We feel there may be many measures of *talent* and hope for future research that seeks and values abilities in all realms.

Note also that the innate capabilities within analytic and holistic modes are not normally understood in a way that allows one to elucidate the method behind the accomplishments. Those who can draw or compute numbers cannot tell you how they arrive at their results, just as most people cannot innately explain our use of the phonemic system or grammar in language comprehension. If we could, then schooling in parsing sentences, spelling, and analyzing narrative would not be the onerous tasks that they are. The fields of grammar and linguistics, as well as art history and aesthetics, are attempts to discover and consciously express underlying semiosic capabilities that are inherently and unconsciously mediated aspects of the experienced world.

Finally, we should once again stress that for every person there is some element of both holistic thinking and analytic thinking present, though in varying levels of dominance. These differences make for very real problems in understanding others, since we all make the assumption that others think in the same way we do. The experience working around the artistic visual thinkers of an art department makes one acutely aware of the difficulty in envisioning another's worldview. In our papers and lectures on the subject, we have used the analogy of the Apple and PC computer platforms, which are constructed out of essentially common material components. The underlying structure and coding of an Apple system is designed for processing images, while PCs are designed mainly around word processing and statistical analysis. Both platforms will accommodate images and text, but not in the same ways. We also find it interesting how computer use is split across our university, the art and math departments preferring Mac computers, while most of all the rest of the campus uses PCs.

While discovering these differences in cognitive mode, I was also beginning to be just a little convinced that what I was looking at had importance not only for human origins, but in understanding human differences in all their forms. I quietly became a bit dangerous, a scientist who is convinced of her view. That can make one quite intolerable in social situations, but for me it served to keep me on track over the years. Still, to continue my look into human origins, my next step was to further my initial supposition about the comparison between Nadia's works and those of the Upper Paleolithic by taking a closer look at the cave paintings of southern France.

WORKS CITED

Grandin, Temple. 1995. *Thinking in Pictures and Other Reports from My Life with Autism.* New York: Doubleday.

Grandin, Temple, and Catherine Johnson. 2005. *Animals in Translation.* Orlando, FL: Harcourt, Inc.

Hermelin, Beate. 2001. *Bright Splinters of the Mind: A Personal Story of Research with Autistic Savants.* Philadelphia: Jessica Kingsley Publishers.

Levinson, Barry, dir. 1988. *Rain Man.* Boston, MA: Guber-Peters Company.

Luria, A. R. 1987. *The Mind of a Mnemonist.* Cambridge, MA: Harvard University Press.

Prince-Hughes, Dawn. 2001. *Gorillas among Us: A Primate Ethnographer's Book of Days.* Tucson: University of Arizona Press.

———. 2004. *Songs of the Gorilla Nation: My Journey through Autism.* New York: Harmony Books.

Sacks, Oliver W. 1995. *An Anthropologist on Mars.* New York: Vintage Books.

Tammet, Daniel. 2007. *Born on a Blue Day: Inside the Extraordinary Mind of an Autistic Savant.* New York: Free Press.

Chapter Six

Art of the Upper Paleolithic

Karen's Story: My experiences in researching the Upper Paleolithic cave paintings provided me with a dilemma exactly counter to the frustrations I experienced in looking for academic works on autism. Instead of finding a limited number of sources, I had the daunting task of sifting through too much data, in search of information relevant to my direction of research. The number of published works on the subject is due to the fact that the paintings captured the attention of the public from the very first discovery in the 1800s. While in the mid-1990s I had to rely on library resources for views of the art, the internet now provides ample methods of accessing the works. Several examples include the Bradshaw Foundation site, which documents early art from various stages of time and from all around the world (see, for instance, Bahn and Vertut 1988); UNESCO's World Heritage Centre site, which includes records of every place designated on their World Heritage List; and the French Ministére de la Culture site, which includes a magnificent virtual tour of the Lascaux cave (links are provided in the works cited for this chapter). Before such resources could be created, the paintings had to go through decades of study to establish their antiquity. This was simply because of the impressive quality of the images and the fact that there is no precursor art showing a development of the skills evident in the images. This suggested to some that the paintings themselves couldn't possibly be as old as initially surmised, and they were actually suspect as authentic elements of the archaeologic record. However, due to the sheer numbers of sites and images that were added to the record in the ensuing years, the association of some of the works to sites with more standard archeological evidence for the period, and the comparable style and skill in evidence in the figurine art associated with the Upper Paleolithic, the cave paintings were finally established as being representative of a critical time period in the development of modern humans (Pfeiffer 1982, 23).

Many volumes provide catalogs of Upper Paleolithic cave images, but each volume also seeks to organize the images into some sort of chronological order. This is the standard method in analysis for the archaeological record, so for each catalog there already existed a rather sophisticated classification system for the larger Upper Paleolithic tool inventory. In addition to the animal representations in the caves, moreover, there often exist, in association with the icons, wholly abstract markings (presumably symbolic rhemes). Leaving aside for the moment consideration of symbolic elements, among the artifactual data recovered at some Paleolithic sites are figurines and small sculpted iconic objects, indicating that imaging technologies in general were also being pursued. These objects are referred to in academic works as mobilary (or portable) art to differentiate them from the parietal (stationary, or literally "off the wall") works that are the cave paintings. The record of mobilary art is extensive and is common to almost all sites within the Upper Paleolithic, regardless of location (Cunliffe 1994; Brantingham, Kuhn, and Kerry 2004). In contrast, the parietal works are for the most part confined to the areas in southern France and northern Spain where the geologic makeup of the region provided the cave contexts that inspired the artists of the time. Preservation in these cave environments was a happy accident, forming an archive of human activity not possible elsewhere. We consider the cave paintings as representative of the era in general, not as a singular "invention" that occurred only in this region. Instead, the region simply provides a serendipitous record of preservation, offering rich data that would otherwise be lost to us, much as the bogs of the British Isles have provided a rich source of data on later European cultures.

The exceptional nature of the Upper Paleolithic art led researchers to comment in what is, for us now, familiar ways. The quality of the art was so exceptional as to not be believed (Pfeiffer 1982, 23; Ucko and Rosenfeld 1967, 33). The images are often superimposed, sometimes to such an extent that individual images are almost impossible to distinguish amid the mass of engraved and painted lines (Ucko and Rosenfeld 1967, 40). To repeat what bears repeating, this overlapping is similar to the composite drawings of Nadia, again suggesting that the creative process of drawing was more important than some presentation for viewing. The realism of the animals depicted in the Upper Paleolithic paintings, in contrast to the stylized, abstract, or symbolic forms of today's tribal art, have an almost live quality to them and a very "modern" style of execution (Donald 1991, 283). In fact, some of the artists of the early modern period were influenced by them (Read 1964, 43). Stephen J. Gould, in a 1996 Natural History article on the cave art, makes the comment that although humans, particularly scientists, are a "contentious lot" who agree on almost nothing, "Every last mother's son and daughter among us stands in reverent awe and amazement before the great cave paintings done by our ancestors in southern and central Europe" (16). The powerful visual impact of the cave art has been noted by the popular press (Hughes 1995, 56). Honour and Fleming (1995, 7), in their general introduction to the history of art, also attest to the quality of the images:

> For sheer vitality, freedom of hand and sureness of touch, the best of these paintings have rarely been excelled. The bulls at Lascaux, for instance, or the bison at Altamira, or the shaggy horses at Niaux beautifully catch an essential "animality," suggesting not only form and texture but also gait and physical presence with an astounding economy of means. They are among the most vivid of all paintings of animals.

Or, as John Pfeiffer (1982, 11) put it:

> There is nothing faint or uncertain, however, about the subsequent course of events, the phenomenon of the Upper Paleolithic. Art came with a bang as far as the archaeological record is concerned. There is nothing to foreshadow its emergence, no sign of crude beginnings.

For decades archaeologists worked to devise an order to the chaos that is the record of the parietal works. There seemed to be much evidence for the expected transformation of skill over time, as the images of the walls are quite varied in their refinement of representation. There are incomplete scratches that only hint of an image, there are the famous, gloriously colorful, fully rendered depictions, and there is everything in between (Ucko and Rosenfeld 1967, 48). So, it would only make sense that a pattern would emerge that would point to a transformation over time. Attempts were undertaken to elucidate developmental trends via relations among: cave locations, image locations within the caves, stylistic variations, subject matter, and relative ages derived from overlapping images. Despite decades of work and a plethora of theories based on technique or structure and meaning, no proposed sequences received widespread support (Gould 1996, 73; Ucko and Rosenfeld 1967, 72–79, 238). There are thousands and thousands of images spread among hundreds of cave sites all produced over tens of thousands of years of the Upper Paleolithic record. Yet, as Honour and Fleming (1995, 11) noted:

> A kind of unity can, however, be discerned in Paleolithic art, a generic similarity between the animals painted or engraved on stone and between the carved figures which have been found in many widely separated places. On the other hand, it is not possible to trace in them any lines of development such as may be seen in the increasingly subtle working of flint arrow-heads and hand-axes.

One should consider that the analytic methods used in determining the progression of lithic technology cannot be applied to the art. There is technological invention involved in producing the paintings: the development of the paints themselves or the burin stone tools for incising the rock walls and, of course the development of the lighting source, the lamps that allowed deeper access to the cave's inner realms. With stone-tool technology, the production of each artifact must be consistent with tried-and-true methods for the successful completion of a useful implement. But, for the art itself, which has no obvious utilitarian function, there are no real constraints on the production of the image. Only the individual artist's particular motivation defines the end product. Like some of Nadia's works, the positioning of images on top of other images suggests that it is the process of producing the image as an instance, a token of the act of creating the icon, that holds importance to the artist, not some overall result beyond the moment of its creation. The iconic representations of animals are not created to be seen. They were not placed within habitation sites and were often produced in the most inhospitable situations deep within the cave complex. The reasoning behind the construction of the representation would be entirely personal, or part of a group dynamic. But, in essence, the work would represent one person's thoughts and *capabilities*. In the end, the huge variations and sheer numbers of images left standard analytical methods incapable of producing a viable chronological development of this new element of the archaeological record.

The story of the art grew murkier still as new caves continued to be discovered. And each new discovered panel of images stirred the public reaction and continues to do so to this day. At the time of my initial research, the most recent, and one of the most impressive, finds was still making headlines, Chauvet Cave near Avignon, France (Hughes 1995, 53). This discovery was quite important, not only for the quality of the images, but the fact that their study could be conducted with the precautions of the latest methods in archaeological research. Many of the past sites had been disturbed too quickly and data lost in the rush to make an impression. And the images themselves were being lost simply by being subjected to the air and light of the admiring public. Chauvet Cave would be accessed only by researchers with measures taken to preserve the conditions that had kept the works intact over the millennia. And, for the first time there were dating methods employed on the works themselves through samples of the charcoals used in their creation. The images at Chauvet, though regarded as highly refined, were found to be some of the oldest in the record (Chauvet, Deschamps, and Hillaire 1996, 121–24; Gould 1996, 73). The quest for the standard method of "skills developed over time" had to be put aside for the cave art of the Upper Paleolithic. Indeed, studies of the art of later periods reinforces the conclusion that simplified or schematic representations follow the Upper Paleolithic development of naturalistic visual art, consistent with our larger argument on the later emphasis of the analytic mode of cognition in Homo sapiens.

Invariably, each of the studies of cave paintings also includes suppositions on why the images were created in the first place, generally focused around notions of ritual and hunting magic. But for our purposes the significance of the art lies in the fact that it was created in the first place. The existence of the images provides a more explicit indication of the cognitive patterns of the people of the Upper Paleolithic than is suggested by the complexities in the stone-tool technologies referenced in Chapter 3. What the tool assemblages imply about the level of analytical thinking is confirmed by the cave images. The act of creating an image suggests a meaning behind it. The figurative depictions are primarily icons and are thus at least partially interpretable as such, but uninterpretable rhematic symbols also appear on the cave walls, which indicate some association of arbitrary meanings behind the works (see also Pfeiffer 1982, 144). Considering the extent of effort involved in developing the technologies behind the creation of the art, the presence of purely symbolic markings, and the personal journeys undertaken within the rarefied atmosphere of the inner cave environment, the whole record reflects a highly charged significance and meaning. These caves were visited for the purposes of recording ideas, a tradition which held for tens of thousands of years. The sites themselves must have been imbued with meaning, since the caves are not the only ones in the region. There are thousands of caves in that part of Europe, while the number containing the images is only a few hundred (Pfeiffer 1982, 118). Moreover, recent research is unveiling substantial examples of Paleolithic cave art in Eastern Europe, including sites in Croatia that some researchers suggest to be contemporary with Chauvet Cave. But the Croatian paintings may only date to perhaps around twenty thousand years ago (the date suggested for the cave's formation) or perhaps earlier, once better dating can be established (see University of Southampton 2019). More significant is the recent definitive dating of rhematic symbols to at least 64,800 years ago at three caves in Spain (Wong 2018), a date well into the Middle Paleolithic and almost certainly prior to the appearance of Upper Paleolithic humans in the region. The appearance of such marks made by Neanderthal people is not surprising, but it also does not suggest that those populations shared equal cognitive adaptations to Upper Paleolithic people, especially given the absence of the realistic animal depictions at that date, as well as other comparative evidence relating to Middle and Upper Paleolithic populations. As with lithic technology, however, we may now firmly attest some similarities of capacities in the broad process leading to higher-level symbolling behavior.

Once the notion of variations in cognitive style enters into the picture, much of the enigmatic nature of the phenomenon of art during the Upper Paleolithic falls away. The art that comes in "with a bang," then, does not have to be forced from a *supposed* era of experimentation on other media that did not survive over time (Pfieffer 1982, 11; Gould 1996, 8). If you take into account the differentiations behind the cognitive styles of analytic and holistic thought, the images begin to make sense as something created by individuals who are taking on the thought processes of the analytical mind, seeing connections between the actions involved in the artwork with other aspects of their existence, while the holistic mode is still pervasive enough to provide the visual acuity evident in the elegance of the iconic images. The Upper Paleolithic, then, preceded in part by Middle Paleolithic rhematic cave markings, represents a turning point—albeit a protracted one—during which the two cognitive styles are in balance, neither one taking precedence over the other, but indicating a significant step for the continued elaboration of the analytical mode through time.

WORKS CITED

Bahn, Paul G., and Jean Vertut. 1988. *Images of the Ice Age*. New York: Facts on File, Inc.

Bradshaw Foundation, www.bradshawfoundation.com.

Brantingham, P. Jeffrey, Steven L. Kuhn, and Kristopher W. Kerry. 2004. *The Early Upper Paleolithic beyond Western Europe*. Berkeley: University of California Press.

Chauvet, Jean-Marie, Eliette Brunel Deschamps, and Christian Hillaire. 1996. *Dawn of Art: The Chauvet Cave, the Oldest Known Paintings in the World*. Translated by Paul G. Bahn. New York: Harry N. Abrams, Inc.

Cunliffe, Barry. 1994. *The Oxford Illustrated Prehistory of Europe*. Oxford: Oxford University Press.

Donald, Merlin. 1991. *Origins of the Modern Mind: Three Stages in the Evolution of Culture and Cognition*. Cambridge, MA: Harvard University Press.

Gould, Stephen J. 1996. "Up against a Wall." *Natural History* 7: 16–22 and 70–73.

Honour, Hugh, and John Fleming. 1995. *The Visual Arts: A History*, 4th ed. Englewood Cliffs, NJ: Prentice-Hall.

Hughes, Robert. 1995. "Behold the Stone Age." *Time*, February 13: 52–62.

Ministére de la Culture (France), http://archeologie.culture.fr/lascaux/en.

Pfeiffer, John E. 1982. *The Creative Explosion: An Inquiry into the Origin of Art and Religion*. New York: Harper and Row.

Read, Herbert. 1964. *A Concise History of Modern Sculpture*. New York: Oxford University Press.

Ucko, Peter J., and Andree Rosenfeld. 1967. *Paleolithic Cave Art*. New York: McGraw-Hill.
UNESCO's World Heritage Centre, https://whc.unesco.org/en/list/310/video.
University of Southampton. 2019. "Press Release: Archaeologists Identify First Prehistoric Figurative Cave Art in the Balkins." April 10. https://www.sciencedaily.com/releases/2019/04/190410120604.htm.
Wong, Kate. 2018. "Ancient Cave Paintings Clinch the Case for Neanderthal Symbolism." *Scientific American* 318: 2.

Chapter Seven

Empirical Corroboration

Karen's Story: With foundational research working to support my initial ideas, and this new element of cognitive modes working as a means of understanding evolutionary change, I wrote the first chapters of my thesis emphasizing the need to apply the designations of mode in order to properly interpret the archaeological record. I presented them to my mentor in the psychology department and encountered the next strange and confirming "accident" for my ideas on human origins. Dr. Bruce Dunn met with me to talk about my work and was excited about the direction I was taking, particularly since it happened to jibe completely with his own experimental studies. It turned out that he could provide experimental support for my thoughts on the visual and sequential modes of cognition. He told me, "You do realize that is what I have been working on in my lab for several years." The needed record of data to back my purely suppositional interpretation was literally at my fingertips.

I was secretly embarrassed and abashed at my apparent ignorance of Dunn's published works. I knew, generally, that he worked in research involving EEG studies on people engaging in high-level cognition. This was well beyond what most psychologists attempt with EEG studies, which usually involve simply reading lists of words or other low-level cognitive tasks. Dr. Dunn's subjects were reading not just compete sentences, but poetry. Still, I must admit that I had not concerned myself with the possible results of that work.

I was quite amazed, then, when I read the reprint of a journal article he presented to me and found that not only was he looking at differences in cognitive style, holistic and analytic, but he was demonstrating the variations in current populations in very real and measurable terms. At this point I was elated that my work on language origins could be supported so eloquently. But now, after many years of work on the subject, I have finally come to recognize the tremendous coincidence this represented. Subsequent searches of the journals on psychological research indicated that Dunn and his close colleagues were the only scientists in his field pursing this topic in this way. And, unfortunately, this avenue has never been taken up by others—even those who coauthored his publications—after he was lost to us to cancer only a few years later. I had hoped to see his ideas established and expanded upon by neuroscientists elsewhere.

My good fortune for my own work was twofold. Not only did I happen to have the needed research in my own back yard, I was actually under Dunn's guidance for my own research. His work in this area was confined to a short time frame, as well as being immediately available to me. I should have recognized the enormity of this gift back then, but it took years of reflection for me to fully comprehend the significance of our serendipitous connection. It is partially my eventual, though overdue, appreciation of this and other gifts of happenstance surrounding my work that has led me to write this book. I feel it is not only the message I am presenting here that is important, but the sense of responsibility to acknowledge and share.

DUNN'S METACONTROL IN COGNITION

The article Bruce Dunn provided as background, "Metacontrol: A Cognitive Model of Brain Functioning for Psychophysiological Study of Complex Learning" (Dunn et al. 1992), was a culminating work offering a synthesis of several years of research on the subject (see Dunn 1983, 1985; Dunn et al. 1981, 1987). The paper set up an excellent summation of what is, of course, a highly complex variable in human cognition. Once one accepts the notion of the variation between holistic and analytic thought, one comes to realize that the reality in human populations goes well beyond a simple one-line continuum. Individuals do not simply represent one or the other in style but offer a complex of variations not only between individuals, but even within individuals.

Broad human variations exist, however, even though the basic brain ontogeny in mammals shows remarkable consistency of process in the earlier stages of development. While we will stress the stimulus-rich emergence of cognition in the postnatal environment of human infants, it is important to note that significant ontogenic development of the brain proceeds before birth, including neurogenesis, neuronal migration, histogenic cell death, and early synaptogenesis. J. P. Bourgeois (2001, 27–28) reviews the role of these processes involved in cortical development, comparing studies on the rat, cat, macaque, and humans. Still, by midway through gestation in humans, apes, and the macaque, neuronal networks begin to be fine-tuned with "experience-expectant" mechanisms, and later "experience-dependent" processes that continue through early childhood and culminate with a spate of synaptic pruning at puberty. Bourgeois (24) uses the term synaptic "decline" for this process that continues more slowly throughout the lifespan. Among other Hominoidea, similar postnatal mechanisms exist, though most of the absolute brain growth in these species occurs mainly before birth. Thus, what we can say about human ontogeny we can extend only partially to ape development, the relative differences being functions of the timing of gestation, acquisition of motor independence, and puberty.

In addition to the synaptic growth and decline sequence, the process of *myelination* (growth of surface membranes formed by glial cells that wrap around axons) is even more significant (Rosenvweig, Leiman, and Breedlove 1999, 33). This fatty tissue makes up the "white matter" of the brain, as opposed to the "gray matter" comprised of neurons and axons. As Ricardo Sampaio and Charles Truwit (2001, 35) explain, myelination occurs from about:

> 12–14 weeks of gestation in the spinal cord and continues well into the third and fourth decades of life in the intra-cortical fibers of the cerebral cortex; but the most important and dramatic changes occur between mid-gestation and the end of the second postnatal year, with myelination accounting in large part for the large gain in brain weight, which more than triples during this period.

Myelination reinforces synaptic connections by making the electrochemical processes more efficient, thus serving to "set" circuitry based upon a combination of standard maturation patterns as well as novel sensory experience. As a Primate species with a long period of gestation and dependent childhood development, even though many basic dedicated cell clusters are established early on, the myelination process may well strongly influence balances of holistic and analytic processing in the individual.

Turning to Bruce Dunn's "metacontrol" model of holistic and analytic brain functions, we note that the studies were completed on adult subjects whose general neurophysiology was well established. The Dunn et al. metacontrol model pulls particularly from research involving electroencephalography (EEG) testing and topographic EEG mapping using event-related potential (ERP) activity, summarized in Dunn and Reddix 1991 (460–67). The EEG studies measured the amount of alpha activity (8–13 Hz) recorded in the cortex during cognitive processing. Low alpha production relates to analytic processing and high alpha activity to the holistic style (for a summary of the research establishing the specific alpha-activity parameters for distinguishing the two cognitive modes, see McKay et al. 2003, 2). In the 1991 article, Dunn et al. worked from the assumption that everyone uses both analytical and holistic modes in thought and that some typically use one more than the other. Participants were separated into two groups, analytics and holistic, based on their baseline alpha production. Their EEG activity was recorded from two sites, one on each hemisphere, left and right, during reading tasks designed to require analytical or holistic processing. The analytical example was represented by an expository text, a passage explaining the relative merits of breeder reactors for generating electricity, and the holistic represented by two poems, one descriptive and one argumentative. The high level of metaphor and imagery within a descriptive poem was meant to represent a text requiring holistic processing, while the argumentative poem's more logical structure should provide a more median task involving both holistic and analytic processing. In addition to the EEG readings, the subjects were asked to provide recall information on what they read and were scored on accuracy. The results affirmed the notion that the baseline alpha activity distinctions on style were consistent with the reading performance recordings, indicating that the alpha activity was a "reliable physiological correlate of modal processing" (276). Those participants designated as analytic showed a greater accuracy in recall of the expository passage, while the holistic individuals showed greater accuracy of recall of the descriptive poem. They did, however, find a significant variant in recall with gender, in that the female participants whether designated analytic or holistic showed equivalent scores in recall of the descriptive poem. Finally, the results also indicated no differentiation between the two hemispheric sites, which suggests that the two styles are not relegated to the left and right hemispheres, as previously assumed.

The metacontrol model presented in the 1992 article by Dunn and his collaborators is based loosely in the Levy and Trevarthen (1976) notion of a metacontrol system working from the lower brain areas. Levy and Trevarthen proposed an executive control system in an attempt to explain inconsistencies on research into the left-brain/right-brain hypothesis for analytic and sequential thinking. Dunn and his group agreed with the idea of a controlling mechanism stemming from the more primitive areas of the brain, though not related to hemispheric differentiation, citing more current research demonstrating that both hemispheres of the neocortex show analytic and holistic capabilities (Sergent 1982). Instead, they considered a control from the lower brain areas would serve to establish a basis for its apparent importance in emotions, memory, and cognition as noted in Mishkin and Appenzeller (1987). For Dunn et al., the metacontrol theory represents (1992, 457):

> a model of how the brain functions dynamically and constructively to create the mind and how the mind and the brain interact with one another. . . . The metacontrol model argues that the prime initiator, or executive, of cognition dwells in the lower brain areas, or metacontrol system, which includes the limbic system, thalamus, hypothalamus and other structures. The higher brain systems, including the brain's lobes and cortex, are seen to interact with the metacontrol system to produce human thought and action.

Within this metacontrol model, Dunn and his team consider the analytic and holistic modes of cognition to be the strategies utilized to "reproduce or reconstruct information" (459). They also surmised that (462):

> Although we have been able to reliably identify two extreme processing styles using EEG alpha measurements, we do not believe that analytics and holistics are extreme styles on a single continuum.... Theoretically, people can be classified as high analytic/low holistic, high holistic/low analytic, high analytic/high holistic, or low analytic/low holistic.

Dunn's work served to reinforce my nascent ideas for the evolution of language in more ways than one. First, there is a confirmation of the analytical and holistic dichotomy through a physiological foundation. The dynamic function of the metacontrol model works well with Peirce's dynamic aspect of semiosis and the notion of a perfusion of signs. Second, the control stemming from neural networks of the lower brain system would stand for elements of cognition foundational to intelligence at its inception in evolutionary terms. And, finally, the hypothesized dual continua would have to be a necessary component of a surmised time-differentiated change of dominance for two cognitive styles.

However, a closer look at Dunn's research brought to light yet another example of the constraints inherent in the academic approach to understanding the holistic mode. In 2003 McKay, Fischler, and Dunn conducted an experiment essentially repeating the methods of the Dunn et al. 1991 work, but this time taking EEG readings on nineteen different sites in order to identify possible "complex topographic patterns of baseline alpha that might be more clearly associated with performance on the analytic and wholistic passages" (5). Working from results published on a 1988 study by Davidson, they sought to establish evidence of differentiation across cognitive styles during reading activity on anterior sites versus posterior sites and to confirm lack of significant differences across left and right hemispheres. Their results, however, demonstrated no differentiation in alpha activity across any sites recorded, either across hemispheres or anterior to posterior. The baseline alpha activity that determined the cognitive style for an individual remained relatively constant throughout the study (15). Cognitive style seems to be pervasive for an individual and not subject to variation during cognitive activity.

Also, this study failed to demonstrate a difference in performance via recall data for the analytics or holistics with the poetry passage. While there was a discernable difference in recall scores for the expository passage favoring those designated as analytic, the variation of recall on the poetry passage were essentially the same across both styles (McKay et al. 2003, 15). In summary, they surmised that other elements not accounted for in the experimental design must influence understanding and recall (16), "Clearly, there are many other factors, some motivational, some informational or experiential, that determine what a person will learn and remember from a prose passage."

However, we consider the unexpected results to stem from a basic misunderstanding of the holistic mode at the outset, beginning with the initial defining characteristics noted in the article's introductory section. Citing a work by Riding and Cheema (1991), they state that the styles involve two dimensions: "(1) a preference for *analytic* versus *wholistic* processing, and (2) a preference for *verbal*, conceptual modes of representation, versus *imagery* and visuospatial forms of representation." For their current work they chose to concentrate on the analytic/holistic dichotomy. The method section of the 1991 article (Dunn et al. 277) outlines an extensive amount of analysis that went into selecting the poetry passages used in both the 1991 and 2002 experiments. A series of poems, each considered to be either descriptive or argumentative, were then scored on imagery, metaphor, and argument content; then the measure of centrality of each (relevance to the central theme of the poem). And, each were also scored on logical structure and the use of concrete and abstract word usage. The scoring served to establish a hierarchy of most argumentative to most descriptive in order to select a poem with high holistic properties for use in the study.

In terms of setting up a study looking at analytic versus holistic cognitive activities, we find the selection of poetry to be an inadequate stimulus for the holistic mode, even one determined to have holistic properties. The error, we have come to see, is in making the assumption that the styles can be divided into two aspects and can be judged separately on them. Instead, the holistic processing must depend on imagery and visuospatial forms. Descriptive poetry may represent a highly holistic form of language, but it is still a form of language per se, which is, as we have proposed, the ultimate in analytic and sequential processing. Poetry, then, could at best only serve for experimental purposes as a mediating activity between the two extremes. An essentially visual task would best suit to truly test the differences in performance for the two cognitive modes. In this instance, the *analytic* methods of the researchers worked against their objectives. And, more importantly, for a point we will return to again in later chapters, there are times when the analytic tendency to divide and segment can become counterproductive.

Dunn's work nonetheless demonstrates that an element of holistic thought is still pervasive in human populations, but also reveals, given the basic commitment of humans to language as communication, that the visual aspect of thought has been largely undervalued in the educational and academic canon. We surmise that this oversight comes from the general human inability to recognize idiosyncrasies of our own thought processes. Humans may be particularly good at discerning emotions and distress in others, but we fail to understand the variations in the underlying processes behind them.

This becomes clear when we consider some of the early research into the Upper Paleolithic paintings. Archaeologists have often been unable to come to terms with the skill of these early artists, a problem even shared by an art historian, E. H. Gombrich (1956). Gombrich's work sought to establish a narrative of art in its entirety, beginning with paleoart, though his works really concentrated only on the history of Western art. Still, this historian was not only unable to recognize the inherent abilities of the early works, he also didn't adequately represent the underlying visual abilities of classic artists such as DaVinci or Michelangelo. He went so far as to hypothesize that various modern methods used in "teaching" drawing, the background grid for example, had to underlie the final output of classic works (146–241, 347). To us this represents the perfect example of the natural wordsmith encountering a natural visual artisan, since Gombrich and other academics express little sensitivity for the visual memory, applying analytical arguments to create an elaborate schema as *explanation of what they do not see.*

Once one takes into consideration the visual mode as a manifestation of holistic processing, one may account for the art of the Upper Paleolithic through the simple notion that holistic consciousness was more prevalent in human populations during this time frame. Rather than having a population with only a few "gifted" individuals who could produce the fine images, it is more likely the case that most were capable of producing the images, while at the same time the burgeoning analytic mind had found a need for the depictions.

So, why did the exemplary art of the Upper Paleolithic begin and end there? Remember, as we noted in the previous chapter, there were gradations in quality, but the more elegant images were found to be the oldest. We suggest that the analytic mode was undergoing a change toward primacy during the Paleolithic as a whole, and that the fundamental state among the early Hominidae involves the dominance of the holistic mode, as Grandin surmises for all animals. This supposition is supported by psychological researchers. For example, Kemler Nelson's conclusion (as quoted in Beyler and Schmeck 1992, 710), after reviewing studies on the two modes of processing, noted "that holistic processing . . . may be frequent, fundamental, and primitive in human cognition." We agree. We argue, moreover, that there must have occurred in the development of the human species a gradual increase in the analytic mind toward the point at which it becomes the dominant mode. We devote other chapters to our ideas on how this came about, but for now, we note that the Upper Paleolithic points to a time when both modes of thought were in balance. Analytic thought was allowing connections to be recognized, and this new way of modeling connections to surroundings became important. Acknowledging connections became part of behavior, providing a reason to express oneself at a time when humans were particularly capable of doing that in the visual mode.

As I have said before, the balance of the analytic and visual modes seems a simple solution to the mystery of the onset of the Upper Paleolithic art. This simple solution does seem to explain much confusion in an elegant fashion. Still, if what I am suggesting is the case, then the end of the Upper Paleolithic art must be explained in the same fashion. The loss of such exceptional art in the archaeological record must signal the point at which the analytic mode begins its dominance in human populations, and there should be evidence to indicate this. When I went out to verify this point, I came upon the next coincidental aspect of my studies.

WORKS CITED

Beyler, Jane, and Ronald Ray Schmeck. 1992. "Assessment of Individual Difference in Preferences for Holistic-Analytic Strategies: Evaluation of Some Commonly Available Instruments." *Educational and Psychological Measurement* 51 (3): 709–19.

Bourgeois, J. P. 2001. "Synaptogenesis in the Neocortex of the Newborn: The Ultimate Frontier for Individuation." In *Handbook of Developmental Cognitive Neuroscience*, edited by Charles A. Nelson and Monica Luciana, 23–34. Cambridge, MA: MIT Press.

Davidson, Richard J. 1988. "EEG Measures of Cerebral Asymmetry: Conceptual and Methodological Issues." *International Journal of Neuroscience* 39: 79–81.

Dunn, Bruce R. 1983. *Psychobiological Model of Cognitive Processing*. Unpublished manuscript, The University of West Florida, The Laboratory for Studies in Neurocognition, Pensacola.

Dunn, Bruce R. 1985. "Bimodal Processing and Memory from Text." In *Psychophysiological Aspect of Reading and Learning*, edited by V. Rentel, S. Corson, and B. Dunn. New York: Gordon & Breach Science Publishers.

Dunn, Bruce R., David Andrews, Marlin L. Languis, Denise Dunn, and N. Gibson. 1987. "Electrophysiological Correlates of Information Processing: Implications for Educational Diagnosis." In *Education, the Brain, and Individual Differences in Learning*, chaired by P. Nauor. Symposium conducted at the annual meeting of the American Educational Research Association, New Orleans, April.

Dunn, Bruce R., Denise Dunn, David Andrews, and Marlin L. Languis. 1992. "Metacontrol: A Cognitive Model of Brain Functioning for Psychophysiological Study of Complex Learning." *Educational Psychologist* 27(4): 455–71.

Dunn, Bruce R., Jay E. Gould, and Michael Singer. 1981. *Cognitive Style Differences in Expository Prose Recall* (Tech. Rep. No. 210). Urbana: University of Illinois, Center for the Study of Reading (ERIC Document Reproduction Service No. ED 205 922).

Dunn, Bruce R., and Michael D. Reddix. 1991. "Modal Processing Style Differences in the Recall of Expository Text and Poetry." *Learning and Individual Differences* 3: 265–93.

Gombrich, Ernst H. 1956. *Art and Illusion: A Study in the Psychology of Pictorial Representation* (Bollingen Series XXXV/5). Washington: Pantheon Books.

Levy, Jerre, and Cowlyn Trevarthen. 1976. "Metacontrol of Hemispheric Function in Human Split-Brain Patients." *Journal of Experimental Psychology: Human Perception and Performance* 2: 299–312.

McKay, Michael T., Ira Fischler, and Bruce R. Dunn. 2003. "Cognitive Style and Recall of Text: An EEG Analysis." *Learning and Individual Differences* 14: 1–21.

Mishkin, Mortimer, and Tim Appenzeller. 1987. "The Anatomy of Memory." *Scientific American* (June): 80–89.

Riding, Richard, and Indra Cheema. 1991. "Cognitive Styles—An Overview and Integration." *Educational Psychology* 11: 193–215.

Rosenvweig, Mark R., Arnold L. Leiman, and S. Marc Breedlove. 1999. *Biological Psychology: An Introduction to Behavioral, Cognitive, and Clinical Neuroscience*. Sunderland, MA: Sinauer Associates Incorporated.

Sampaio, Ricardo, and Charles Truwit. 2001. "Myelination in the Developing Human Brain." In *Handbook of Developmental Cognitive Neuroscience*, edited by Charles A. Nelson and Monica Luciana, 35–44. Cambridge, MA: MIT Press.

Sergent, Justine. 1982. "The Cerebral Balance of Power: Confrontation or Cooperation?" *Journal of Experimental Psychology: Human Perception and Performance* 8: 253–72.

Chapter Eight

Art of the Mesolithic

Karen's Story: Working from my supposition about the transformation of cognitive styles and Upper Paleolithic art, I began to look at the archaeological record for the immediately subsequent period, the European Mesolithic. Surprisingly, I had to look no further than our own library to find what I needed. We have, over the years, accumulated a large collection on the subjects within anthropology that my husband taught and others that were purchased based on my particular interests. Therefore, we have a number of volumes on early art and specifically works on the Paleolithic art of southern France. One particular volume is André Leroi-Gourhan's seminal work on the cave paintings, The Dawn of European Art *(1980). This book was published in a series with another work that looked at art from areas adjacent to the caves in France, Antonio Beltrán's* Rock Art of the Spanish Levant *(1982).*

The artworks of the caves of the Upper Paleolithic, and evidently the caves themselves, were eventually abandoned (Cunliffe 1994, 78; Pfeiffer 1982, 149). The culture producing them is thought to have died out or moved on, due to climatic and environmental pressures stemming from the close of the last ice age (Cunliffe 1994, 75–78). What then follows in the artistic record may be a progression of sorts, but working, surprisingly for art historians, away from naturalism and toward schematics.

The Spanish Levant is a low mountainous region that runs along the eastern coast of Spain. Within this area over the years archaeologists have discovered more than seven hundred sites that have been designated on UNESCO's list of World Heritage Sites. However, there are many more sites that have been requested to be included on the list (Hernández and Hernández 2013, 26). Beltrán's 1982 analysis dealt only with 112 sites (10). The paintings and a few etched works occur on low overhangs and shallow recesses across upper escarpments of the region. These sites run all the way from Huesca in the north, just below the Pyrenees, to Cadiz in the far south. The paintings are not located in deep caves as in the Paleolithic, but are in what is more appropriately designated rock shelters (Beltrán 1982, 12). The shelters have not provided living sites in association that could clearly indicate a time frame for the art (Beltrán 1982, 71). Nor do the open-air positions of the paintings allow for reliable carbon dating of the pigments. From the beginning, the sites were problematic in terms of dating, and this remains an issue even today (for example, see Roldán et al. 2018; or Ruiz et al. 2012).

Dating for these sites, then, must stem from analysis of the artworks themselves. Their characteristics and subject matter have placed them in the Mesolithic era, a period between the Upper Paleolithic realism and the symbolism of the Neolithic. The dates that define this period vary with the areas studied, but generally run from about 15,000 to 5,000 BP. Within this time frame the particular sites selected by the people of the time were of sufficient significance to warrant their repeated use; there are many different depictions placed through time, and some images even show evidence of repainting (Beltrán 1982, 57).

As with the Upper Paleolithic art, images representing the Spanish Levant can be experienced virtually with online sources, such as the websites at the Spanish Ministry of Culture and Sports and at Venamicasa. Each wall of painting within the Spanish Levant consists of a tangle of figures that include three types, designated as naturalistic, stylized, and schematic:

a. The naturalistic images are the single, static animal figures that suggest the images of the Upper Paleolithic. They are larger than any other images (about one meter in length, Beltrán 1982, 18), but are smaller than the images of the caves of France. The largest of the Spanish Levant depictions are about the size of the smallest of their precursor images (Beltrán 1982, 65). Also, they are invariably only a single color (Beltrán 1982, 21), never reaching the level of the impressive multicolor masterpieces we see in the best of the works from the Upper Paleolithic.
b. As an important diversion from the older style of works, there are multiple much smaller figures (sometimes only a couple of centimeters high) that occur in and around the naturalistic animal figures. These are stylized figures of humans in groups and in action. Although the images are much like stick figures, they skillfully indicate movement through variation of their arm and leg positions and body angles. As Beltrán (1982) notes, "the figures are now governed by different pictorial conventions: drawn with continuous strokes which are linear, though with inflection and flourishes, to achieve an impressionistic rendering of parts of the body and the movement which pervades the scenes" (21). The multiple figures work together

to express a scene of action, the telling of a story. They seem primarily to represent hunting activities, as there are animals included and the human figures appear to be wielding bows and arrows. There are other scenes that seem more pastoral or that represent possible dancing, and even scenes that suggest clashes between groups.

c. Finally, some of the sites within the Spanish Levant include painted schematic designs that do not represent any form of iconic image, and so are purely symbolic in nature.

Given the varying types of images that occur in the Spanish Levant, scholars expected that careful analysis would demonstrate the development over time from naturalistic, to stylized, to schematic. This would be established by noting overlapping images within the friezes that exhibited more than one type. Surprisingly, this sequence of development over time could not be clearly demonstrated definitively. Instead, some exceptions to the expected rule were found. There were occasions where the naturalistic animal figures clearly overlaid stylized action scenes (Beltrán 1982, 27) and examples of schematic symbols underlying the naturalistic figures (70). These findings were one more real deterrent to the dating of the sites and added yet another enigmatic element to the record for early art. Despite years of continued research and tremendous increase in the numbers of rock art sites discovered, the record of the art continues to confuse the issue of human evolutionary development to this day (for example, see Hernández and Hernández 2013).

However, from our perspective focused on transformations in cognitive style, this body of data offers another way in which our argument about cognitive evolution can clear muddied waters. The presence of narrative and emotive scenes in Mesolithic contexts, in conjunction with images that are in continuity with Paleolithic style, shows clearly that the Mesolithic is a further step in the direction of more prominent analytic thought. The art of the Mesolithic is not simply a conversion of ideas, as one technology of representation replaces another. This is not a simple case of new ideas taking hold and replacing old. In our confusing modern world of constant invention and movement of the times, we have come to expect this kind of novelty. But, cultural transformations occur at breakneck speed in comparison to the transformations of biology. And what we are observing with the Mesolithic is a biological transformation. This is a case of the population increasingly gaining analytical consciousness, which in turn is reflected in artistic works. Even though this is a relatively short era in the story of human evolution, it still proceeds over twice the length of time of our modern era. The move from a dominant visual mode to a primarily analytic one, indeed, must have taken place over an extended length of time. What began in the Upper Paleolithic is still in process during the Mesolithic. The minds that created the meaning and significance to the naturalistic animal figures within their equally significant locations are still very much in play, even as stories are developed that take in narrative and are better served by more simplistic images that aid in preserving a serial development of ideas. We are reminded, here, of the use of storyboarding in the film industry. Additionally, in terms of the schematic elements of the Spanish Levant art, remember that there are already purely symbolic elements represented even at the Upper Paleolithic stage of human artistic invention. But, there came a time when the analytic mode was sufficiently dominant within the population that the ideas and vision of the holistic mode became negligible within the artifactual remains that survive to inform. This is the almost purely symbolic aspect behind the creative expressions of the Neolithic era.

It isn't until the development of complex cultures of "classic" times that the occasional individuals, with what are now looked on as possessing extraordinary and gifted capabilities, became a specialized niche within the broad cultural milieu for the expressions of the visual mode.

Beltrán described a general trend away from the naturalistic images of the Paleolithic and toward the schematicized art of the Neolithic (27):

> We can assert that Levantine art underwent progressive development towards stylization, showing a clear tendency to a conceptual approach in principle and to impressionism in execution. Its forms became ever more flat and angular and the figure more elongated, including those of animals. We find a disproportion between scale of component elements which is characteristic of stylization and of schematic art.

However, Beltrán (1982) did not propose a pure evolution recorded completely in this singular locale, but saw instead the final stages of transformation as more probably the result of influences from lowland areas. Thus, he says the change was a cultural process in which domestication of plants and animals had brought in the Neolithic and the stylized art already established (61, 71, 78). Beltrán (81) concluded his study with the following remarks:

> In our view, Levantine art was developed by an upland hunting people within a defined geographical region and began in epi-paleolithic times. There was perhaps a component of paleolithic tradition, but in its general aspect the art is original and local, with a novelty especially apparent in its representation of the human figure. It lasted throughout the neolithic, then, having passed through a significant evolution, it died out with the arrival of eneolithic schematic art, though slowly, and with some features surviving.

This rationalization, however, is unnecessary in the context of a cognitive interpretation of the art. In fact, rock art comparable to typical Neolithic imagery continues among tribal cultures all the way into our time.

Notably, Pfeiffer (1982, 151) also characterized the rock shelter art as *active*, "teeming with life" in contrast to the relatively static images of the cave paintings. The transformation was noted as moving away from sedate, realistic animals and abstract forms toward energetic scenes of stylized human forms. Further still, Pfeiffer cites Lya Dams (1984), who affirms that emotion apparently now entered into the picture, quite literally (151):

> According to Dams, the earliest Levant figures were done in the Upper Paleolithic style, consisting mainly of large and motionless oxen and bison, an indication that one tradition may have developed directly out of the other. She also notes that pain and distress, rarely depicted in the caves where most animals with spears or arrows in their bodies show no more signs of being in trouble than unimpaled animals, appeared as a prominent feature in the Spanish Levant, the indications being mouths open as if crying out and legs giving way. These signs appeared in quantity starting about 8,000 years ago, raising the usual question of why then—of what changes in lifestyle occurred at that time to make artists include the sufferings of wounded animals in more of their paintings.

One explanation of the changes suggested by both Beltrán and Pfeiffer that seems compelling, given what we know today of the evolutionary process, is that adjustments in the neural connections of the expanded cerebral cortex not only provided the basis for narrative, but were accompanied by new neural links between the cortex and the mid and lower brain centers, thus introducing iconic representations of emotional states. We expect that such adjustments would not appear as a single systemic evolution, but rather as a process involving diverse populations with different elements that contributed to the derived system. In other terms, not all individuals of any population shared equally in the emerging cognitive system, and different populations possessed variable manifestations undergoing local transformations controlled by gene flow and variable constraints of natural, and at this point also cultural, selection. In this situation, the relative importance of analytical thinking over holistic experience was more than the simple introduction of narrative, but also suggests a population becoming "more human" in the terms we understand about ourselves today.

If altering connections within the brain structure allowed for complex emotions, as well as narrative, then once again these surprising data begin to make sense of the particular artistic traditions of the Mesolithic—the moves from natural to stylized and from impassive to affected become understandable.

Building a visual/symbolic, holistic/sequential, affective interpretation for the evolution of internal brain structures presents a model of human intelligence, which truly illustrates the plasticity of the emerging human brain and the cognitive diversity of populations following the Paleolithic. One can easily posit a series of developing connections happening in fits and starts as populations lived through generations, encountered other groups, interbred, and were subject to natural selection. To arrive in evolutionary terms at the consistency with which the developing brain of a modern infant establishes a more or less unified body of connections (Dean 1985, 20–23), there must have been a time when not all of the elements were extant throughout the population. We believe such a period, probably occurring geographically throughout immediate Post-Paleolithic populations, is archaeologically represented at least by the Mesolithic peoples of the Spanish Levant. Inasmuch as the Mesolithic and similar manifestations tend in evolutionary terms to be relatively short, we can view the transition as a rapid equilibrium change in brain physiology. We address this partially in later chapters, but we recognize that we are making a rather bold and complex argument here, and we certainly see this as a fruitful area for expanded research on the biological processes and their associated cultural manifestations.

For the moment, we should state that based on current populations, the implied emerging neural connections conjoin higher-level cortical areas with the basic perceptual regions, and the tendrils eventually delve into the limbic system. This process and structure shapes a mind capable of producing complex associations across almost the entire range of relations between inner and outer worlds, connecting them in time and space. This mind evokes a being who questions, then builds systems of knowledge to reveal answers. But even if not all of the qualities involved in the change from a primarily holistic to a primarily analytic cognitive style happened for everyone equally, or at the same rates in different populations, the impact of the restructuring of the brain to accommodate analytic functions was immense.

Over the millions of years required for the development from pebble tools to the emergence of modern *Homo sapiens*, anthropology has always seen "culture" as driving the hominid experience. Indeed, as our understanding of the fossil record of the early Paleolithic has expanded, so have our academic definitions of culture. The implication for many has been that there was a slow co-evolution of technology and communication capabilities. On the contrary, we suggest the beginnings of language as we know it in the sense of the emergent semiotic argument, and therefore also "culture" as we know it, is a relatively late phenomenon, and is particularly associated with the late Upper Paleolithic. With the Mesolithic, however, we begin to see the rapid culmination of that hominid evolution into a full-blown symbolling animal. Since we associate "language" with our symbolling nature, we may well argue that the developments discussed in this chapter are central to the emergence of "language" as a dominant human system. In many respects, the diversity of cognitive styles we see in today's human populations are depicted in Mesolithic art; the art reflects people becoming more like us, but not yet overwhelmingly "like us" in all of their interests or potentials. Thus, we may anticipate a central part of our argument in suggesting that the earliest "biologically modern" humans did not begin using language as a comprehensive speech system, but we are closer to identifying both the time period and the process through which human language emerged, and its place in the evolution of culture in general. Modern humans still encounter the world primarily though icons and indices, though mediated through the symbolic system of speech. It is difficult for us to imagine a world without words, and some people even say they cannot think of the world in pure iconic signs. Though "icons" are present for everyone, the impact of symbols for the vast majority of people dominates thinking. But even today this is not an "all or nothing" system. We must consider that there was a time when not everyone shared equally in the symbolling processes we think of as "natural."

I was elated, of course, at discovering a final confirming element to my argument on transitions in cognitive style. And, it was the first of many occasions throughout the following years where I realized that this simple idea makes for a completely new way of viewing a whole range of enigmatic problems in academics and seems to provide a unique solution. I became very haughtily repetitive in my reaction to all kinds of research, "That may be confusing to you, but the lack of a clear stylistic development in Mesolithic art makes complete sense to me!"

I was truly convinced I was on to something. And, that feeling of accomplishment served to outweigh my reaction to some coincidental aspects behind encountering the needed material that once again was dropped into my lap, this time in my own home. It was years later, decades really, when we began to envision this volume that the importance of these serendipitous events came to the fore in my thinking and became the basis for how to present our argument here.

Feeling that I had made my point on the place of cognitive styles in the development of the modern humans, I completed my thesis and presented it to Dr. Dunn and the university in completion of my master's degree. I had convinced my colleagues in the psychology department of my argument, but I found the most difficult audience for my ideas was my husband. His thorough grounding in linguistics meant that he was at a very basic level engrossed in the notion that the defining characteristics of human thought were dependent on linguistic thought. This is the major tenet for linguists, that the power of language provided the basis for logic and all other inventions of human culture. What I was proposing, instead, stated that inventive thought was the impetus for language.

Evidence for all the most distinctive and impressive accomplishments of human culture date from a time well after the fully modern skeletal form had been established about two hundred thousand years ago. The assumption that no physiological changes occurred due to the lack of skeletal change spurred the further assumption that all subsequent behavioral changes were the result of cultural invention. But, the cognitive style transformations indicate to me that physiological changes have continued to occur via alterations in neural circuitry and that, simply put, the origins of language stem from the rising importance of the analytical mode. Humans found the impetus for communication in the same way they encountered the impetus for depiction. We humans spoke only after we had something to say. But, as I have indicated, this notion is counter to the basic assumptions of linguistics.

All during my process of research on my thesis, my days were punctuated by arguments (well, discussions that were sometimes heated ones) with Terry. I would go over my whole argument time and again and think I had made my point, then find I would have to start again from scratch during our next discussion. This may have been a bit tedious, but it was excellent practice for writing up my ideas, since writing is not my strong suit and getting across an academic argument does not come easily for me. I have theorized that on the two continua Dr. Dunn surmised for the two cognitive styles, I must come in right in the middle of both. I'm not particularly gifted in either direction. But, then that may make me a little more open to visualizing both.

The point is, I could not seem to get my ideas across in a manner that would thoroughly catch in Terry's mind until he began writing a series of papers on the Peircean concept of sign categories and technology, mentioned in an earlier chapter. Although C. S. Peirce was one of the most prolific academics I have ever encountered (some have devoted their entire career to publishing his works), his definition of his sign categories was relatively terse. We spent many hours discussing them and working up a set of definitions we agreed upon. Those discussions set up a series of examples from within the archaeological record as a means to enhance our communication and understanding of Peirce. This background has dominated the way we have worked together to express the ideas forming this book. In preparation for presenting our ideas on human evolution, we need at this point to provide a more thorough discussion of Peirce.

WORKS CITED

Beltrán, Antonio. 1982. *Rock Art of the Spanish Levant*. Translated by Margaret Brown. Cambridge: Cambridge University Press. (Original work published in Italian as *Da cacciatori ad allevatori l'arte rupestre del Levante Spagnolo* by Editoriale Jaca Book, Milan, 1980.)

Cunliffe, Barry. 1994. *The Oxford Illustrated Prehistory of Europe*. Oxford: Oxford University Press.

Dams, Lya. 1984. *Les Peintures Ruprestres Du Levant Espangnol*. Paris: Picard.

Dean, R. S. 1985. "Foundation and Rationale for Neuropsychological Bases of Individual Differences." In *The Neuropsychology of Individual Differences: A Developmental Perspective*, edited by L. C. Hartlage and C. F. Telzrow, 7–40. New York: Plenum Press.

Hernández, Gemma, and Mauro S. Hernández. 2013. "Rock Art of the Mediterranean Basin on the Iberian Peninsula from El Cogul to Kyoto." *Catalan Historical Review* 6: 11–31, Institut d'Estudis Catalans, Barcelona.

Leroi-Gourhan, André. 1980. *The Dawn of European Art: An Introduction of Paleolithic Cave Painting*. Translated by Sara Champion. Cambridge: Cambridge University Press. (Original work published in Italian as *I Piu' antichi artisti d'Europa* by Editoriale Jaca Book, Milan.)

Pfeiffer, John E. 1982. *The Creative Explosion: An Inquiry into the Origin of Art and Religion*. New York: Harper and Row.

Roldán, Clodoaldo, Sonia Murcia-Mascarós, Esther López-Montalvo, Cristina Vilanova, and Manuel Porcar. 2018. "Proteomic and Metagenomics Insights into Prehistoric Spanish Levantine Rock Art." *Scientific Reports*, July 3. www.nature.com/scientificreports.

Ruiz, Juan F., Antonio Hernanz, Ruth Ann Armitage, Marvin W. Rowe, Ramon Viñas, José M. Gavira-Vallejo, and Albert Rubio. 2012. "Calcium Oxalate AMS ^{14}C Dating and Chronology of Post-Paleolithic Rock Paintings in the Iberian Peninsula, Two Dates from Abrigo de los Oculados (Henarejos, Cuenca, Spain)." *Journal of Archaeological Science* 39: 2655–67.

Spanish Ministry of Culture. http://www.spainisculture.com/en/.

Venamicasa. http://www.venamicasa.com/cultural-activities-for-groups/mediterranean-cave-art/.

Chapter Nine

Signs and Lithic Technology

Terry's Story: As Karen moved beyond her thesis and began publishing more articles on her view of language origins, I had already been engaged in semiotic studies for many years. My work, however, was based in French structuralism, inspired by Ferdinand de Saussure, and post-structuralist writings, especially of Roland Barthes. I was also steeped in the structural linguistic foundations of the American linguist Kenneth Pike. With linguistic and narrative structure as my focus, I had not given serious consideration to the philosophical doctrine of signs laid out by C. S. Peirce. The idea that language establishes human thought was a bias that kept me from realizing the importance of sign categories in all animal behavior, and the importance of iconicity and indexicality as the foundations of symbolic experience and, ultimately, linguistic meaning. When I undertook a deeper study of Peirce, as with all personal paradigm shifts, I experienced a rather complete change of perspective. More importantly, I gained a lexicon for sharing in and expressing the ideas Karen was constantly pushing at me. We had found the basis for a more common understanding and the means of clearly discussing and expressing our mutual interests with each other.

In addition, I found the Peircean categories extremely helpful in resolving some descriptive and analytical issues involved in discussions of stone technology in relation to animal behavior generally. In some respects, that process was aided by encounters with contemporary flint knappers. Specifically, I found that individual knappers could produce the same tools with identical features but had totally different ways of expressing what they were doing in words. We have long understood that flint-knapping requires strong motor skills engaging hand-eye coordination and other kinetic elements. Sometimes, it was not the finished tool that was central to the process, but merely "edges" or the qualities of stone sources, all of which can also be related back to the "physics of rock fracture" that was implicit in core positioning in the hand, or the qualities of the hammer used to extract flakes from a core. Stone-tool production is an "art" or "skill" incipient in muscle memory, requiring constant attention to the serendipitous processes of individual acts, all of which preceded any verbal description or instruction between knappers. And this made sense in terms of the holistic versus analytic dimensions Karen had made central to her work. But with Peirce, I was off and running into old territory with a new set of ideas, and those ideas melded nicely into the information from archaeological treatments of the subject, including notions of "typology" and "functionality." It was time to seek a systematic approach to the subject of artifacts and production processes as "signification" to the primate mind, and to the emerging human mind.

The sign system of Charles S. Peirce was created as an inherently discursive model of semiosis generally, inclusive of anthroposemiosis serving humans as the only "semiotic" animal in our experience—the only species capable of formally observing and commenting on semiosis. Perhaps the most universal aspect of Peirce's system is that it handles meanings created by shared definition (i.e., paradigmatic meanings) as well as those created in the flow of communicative process (i.e., syntagmatic meaning).[1] The Peircean process is also inherently open-ended, comprising an "unlimited semiosis," or the dependence of any sign on foundations of other signs, both immediate and remote in experience. Negotiation of the world happens through a "perfusion of signs," abstracting experience at levels of sensation and perception into salient objects and contexts, and accomplishing this by references to other signs. Ferdinand de Saussure arrived at aspects of meaning generation though his concepts of *langue* and *parole*, but his sign world is much more closed, consistent with his linguistic bias. That said, something akin to unlimited semiosis does show up in the work of later scholars in the continental, evolved Saussurean tradition. With Lacan, the signified becomes itself a signifier of further signifiers in an infinite chain of signification. Likewise, Jacques Derrida's concept of *différance* moves well into Peircean territory. But neither Lacan nor Derrida give much attention to how signs create pragmatic meaning, which in Peirce yields something akin to "definitive" signification. So, the Peircean system offers the advantages of (1) being more conducive to understanding the ongoing, discursive production of meaning and (2) the interplay between paradigm and syntax.

Peirce developed a quite elaborate typology of signs, which we have alluded to briefly in earlier chapters. A few comments are in order before delving too deeply into a consideration of types of signs and sign experience. Though precision with words is always desirable, the degree of preciseness represented by the Peircean typology is not necessary for all instances of semiotic analysis. In fact, in most instances, such usage becomes an exercise in the most tedious pedantry. But following on a recent paper by Floyd Merrell (2007), "Why I Believe Becoming Peircean Is Preferable," we want to consider the powerful utility of Peirce's system. So, for the purposes of this exposition, we will pursue some detailed observations in order to make a few points about sign processes and the applicability of Peirce's system to material and behavioral inquiry. Note also the word "processes," since the dynamic of semiosis serving our semiotic interests drives part of our general interest here.

PEIRCE'S SIGN TYPOLOGY

Peirce's sign classification is based on three trichotomies. These are formed by classifying the sign first on the basis of forms or representamens; that is, on the material form of the sign itself. Second, Peirce categorized the relationships between the representamen and its object (whatever is signified), or how a sign "refers" to a class of potential referents.[2] Third, there is the relationship between representamen and interpretant, which we express as the "meaning here-and-now" of the sign, derived from a range of possibilities.[3] The first trichotomy yields the sign categories: qualisign, sinsign, and legisign; the second: icon, index, and symbol; and the third: rheme or term, dicent or proposition, and argument. The classification has been responsibly discussed in detail in diverse sources, among which here Spinks (1991) and Parmentier (1994) have been very helpful to us, alongside direct consideration of Peirce's writings.

A qualisign is an individual quality taken as a sign, and as such is the foundation of all experience, the initial aspect of "sensation." As a quality, this level of sign can only be encountered and function in an actual manifestation (which could be physical or mental). Some have expressed the qualisign as the "ness" of cognition, as in "redness" or "softness," and so on. A sinsign is an individual instance of something that is comprised of bundled qualisigns and that functions as a sign for someone. In essence, the sinsign carries us to the level of "perception." As individual instance, the sinsign may function as a sign of a unique object, or more likely, it may be an individual token of a general type or law. A sign of general type or law, something generalized out of repetitive encounters in experience, becomes a legisign. Sinsigns that are tokens of legisigns will partake of or manifest the law-like aspects of the legisign of which it is a token, while at the same time being connected with an immediate, finite set of several qualisigns, as in the experience of a particular dog, as an example of the mental "concept of dog." This level of the classification is most important to the apprehension of discreet phenomena as standing out from background, as well as to the recognition of repeated associations, or patterns of experience. Such signs occur prior to any form of symbolic reference and are well attested in the behavior of non-human animals.

These categories of signification are useful in developing an understanding of pre-verbal patterned behavior within our species. Such things as territorial behaviors, patterns in memory and attention, muscle memory for repeated actions, and many other elements of behavior underlie material acquisition and manipulation for stone-tool production and use. Indeed, flint knapping proceeds, even for a modern human, not through a conscious internal symbolling process, but through the sense-perception appreciation of a myriad of lower-level signs. In analysis of the process of knapping, the trajectory toward an end product that may or may not have a "name" is a complex one, rarely spelled out explicitly in speech. Fortunately, the residual signs on the materials, finished products and trash alike, tell something of the story, and so provide a glimpse of the capacities of our pre-human ancestors.

Modern science is based upon the sense in which qualisigns are recognized as relevant and then become integral aspects of experience. But all such signs also exist within a wider field of sign elements, so we must consider the first Peircean triad within his second and third trichotomies, a process which invites the use of more explicit examples. The second triad is the easiest set for most people to grasp and, for many contexts, the one that is of greatest importance. First, the *icon* is a sign that signifies through some sort of systematic relationship or similarity to the object signified. This can include straightforward cases such as pictographic representation or more complex cases such as diagrams or metaphor. Second, the *index* is a sign that signifies through calling attention to the object signified by "pointing" or contiguity, including straightforward cases such as the index finger pointing to an object and less-obvious cases such as metonymy, the speech practice of referring to something by reference to one of its attributes.

Indexical signs may exist as non-specific correlations in the here and now, so an index like "smoke filling a room" may be associated with the experience of heat and visual modulations that come with "fire" in an individual instance. One may encounter something like steam, a fog, or even the explosion of spores from a fungus, as similar experiences, and thus refer to them symbolically with terms like "smoke" or "vapor" or "cloud." But such experiences would not necessarily signify "heat" indexically, though on a purely experiential level the visual/perceptual association may not be different enough to be distinguishable.

Thus, the third term of this trichotomy, the symbol, is a sign that signifies the aggregate experience of a population through time, purely through "convention," allowing for refinements of "meaning" that enhance the specificity of sinsigns and legisigns within the cognitive stream. Symbolic anthropology has tended to focus on highly complex symbols in ritual context, but a more mundane (and quantitatively significant) example of symbolic use would be the words we use so habitually, all of which signify through conventional agreement, and as such are symbols.

Now, consider the second Peircean triad through terms used in studies of implement production, non-verbal animal behavior, animal calls, and human speech (Table 9.1). Virtually all of the pre-symbolic sign types occur throughout the animal kingdom, as well as some incipiently symbolic examples among higher primates, with the caveat that symbols are not habitually used by any species other than humans. What is more useful to our discussion here is the realization that human experience through signs (anthroposemiosis) includes grounding engagement in the pre-symbolic level. Also very useful is the realization that flint knapping makes ample use of indexical signs that occur in the ongoing process of creatively breaking rocks. The knapper is constantly monitoring the results of prior breaks to make decisions on how to proceed toward some specified goal. Indexicality, indeed, is critically important to our understanding of most behavior sequences we regard central to early human technology, and hence also to our interpretation of the archaeological record generally, and especially with respect to language origins.

Table 9.1. Examples of Icon, Index, and Symbol in Different Behavioral Contexts

	Materials	Non-Verbal Behavior	Animal Communication	Human Speech
Icon	a "cutting edge" a tool shape	courting behaviors of birds or fish	species-specific vocalizations	phones
Index	tool attribute such as edge grinding to facilitate hafting	postural stances locomotor variations orientation of a bee's dance visual cues in a circus	gustatory sounds distress calls mating calls learned vocal commands	allophones allomorphs inflections
Symbol	ceremonial axe swagger stick crown	marching dancing rituals	learned manual signs	phonemes morphemes syntagmemes

Peirce's third trichotomy offers the essential basis of logic. The rheme (or *term*) merely signifies possible entities identifiable by some set of qualities (or, qualitative possibility, CP 2, 350). Thus, rhemes are "meanings here and now" that connote some class of things or actions. The dicent, or dicisign, signifies actual existence or entails some sort of proposition about the relation of the object signified to the surrounding world. Rhemes and dicisigns occur as icons and indices, becoming fundamental elements of animal cognition. The argument, however, as Peirce puts it, "is a sign whose interpretant represents its object as being an ulterior sign through a law, namely, the law that the passage from all such premises to such conclusions tends to the truth" (CP 2, 263). Or, paraphrasing Peirce, the argument is a sign of reason, building upon propositions (dicisigns) to express an overarching logical system. Explicit formal logic merely employs rhemes and dicents on the symbolic level as part of the uniquely human repertoire. But prior to any explicit logic, the elements of apprehension and understanding can exist in pre-linguistic thought. As John Deely (1982, 1994) explained anthroposemiosis, the argument involves theorization broadly understood, the formal engagement of the analytic mind with the mind-independent world.

For Peirce, through the precise definitions of the elements in the three triads, it was possible to employ them together to create ten distinct sign categories. In the core of Peirce's classification, for any given sign, there will be an element from each of the trichotomies. All signs have at the same time one sort or another of *representamen*, one sort or another relationship to the *object* signified, and one sort or another *interpretant*. By combining the three trichotomies as attributes, we generate Peirce's ten sign types (Table 9.2).

Table 9.2. Nomenclature of C. S. Peirce's Ten Sign Types

rhematic iconic qualisign	or	qualisign
rhematic iconic sinsign		iconic sinsign
rhematic iconic legisign		iconic legisign
rhematic indexical sinsign		rhematic indexical sinsign
rhematic indexical legisign		rhematic indexical legisign
dicent indexical sinsign		dicent indexical sinsign
dicent indexical legisign		dicent indexical legisign
rhematic symbol *legisign*		rhematic symbol
dicent symbol *legisign*		dicent symbol
argument *symbolic legisign*		argument

The terms in italics are not necessary in the differentiation of the type from other types. That is, the qualisign can only be an icon and is always a rheme: As mere quality, it can only signify through similarity with what is signified, with the similarity being possession of the quality. Thus, the terms rhematic or iconic with reference to a qualisign are superfluous. Similarly, icons can only be rhemes. As signs that signify through attribution of similarity to the object represented, they can signify only qualitatively possible phenomena that may partake of this similarity, and they cannot indicate linkage between the object and surroundings as with the propositional nature of the dicent. The symbol must also always be a legisign. As conventional signs, symbols are not tokens of types as in the sinsign, but general types or conventional law-like things. Finally, arguments are always symbolic (and thus, also always legisigns). As signs that build conclusions about the world that move beyond what is directly given, they are clearly beyond icons and indices—though to the extent that particular arguments say something important about the world, they ultimately build upon simpler iconic and indexical signs.

Turning attention now to Figure 9.1, we may view the three trichotomies in a tiered geometrical array. The graph shows the necessary connections of the ten sign types. As we will elaborate later, since semiosis involves a flow of experience operating at multiple levels, we may emphasize the processual aspect of any experiential situation as moving "up" and "down" the systems as sense and perception engage the world.

The ten general sign types offer an extremely precise and comprehensive way of characterizing behavior, as well as for our purposes here, expressing "how" we interpret the archaeological record as reflecting at times a sense of "symbolic" behavior. Though the terms of the classification may seem overly complex at first, once the basic meanings of the features defining each type are understood, one can experience a much clearer appreciation of behavior, communication, and ultimately language. At the least, in our view, the sign types provide a basis for sharing perspective on these matters that is more complete than any other descriptive system.

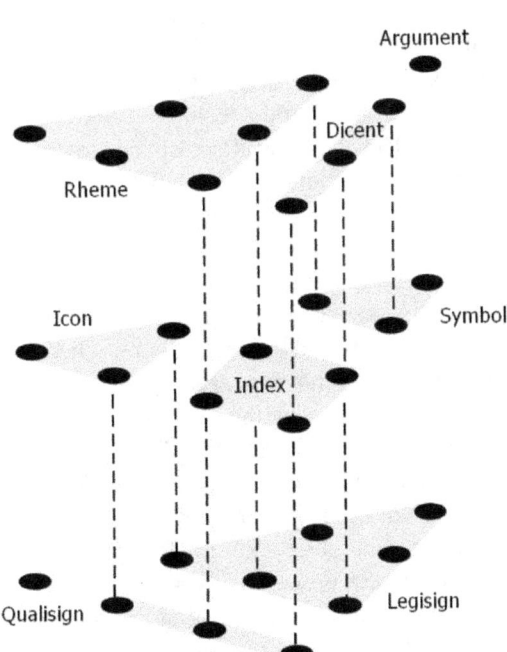

Figure 9.1. The ten sign categories defined by C. S. Peirce, showing the three trichotomies linked in vertical column; the connections emphasize Qualisign and Argument as distinctive "endpoints" of the sign typology. *Source:* T. Prewitt.

PEIRCEAN SIGN TYPES AND STONE TECHNOLOGY

Looking at the ten sign types more closely, we may differentiate them with examples from several areas of behavioral study, and specifically with stone technology. A first point with regard to stone tools is that there need be no necessary close correlation between the tool "types" defined by an archaeologist and those recognized behaviorally by the people who produced them. There have been many ethno-archaeological studies that have made this point. A prime archaeological example would be the Mousterian tool typology introduced by François Bordes. More recent research has argued that there is less difference than Bordes posited between the overall flint-knapping assemblages of Neanderthal and Lower Paleolithic populations, in terms of both production and use. While the form/edge associations of those tools are certainly recognizable, they give undue emphasis to form within entire assemblages. The Middle Paleolithic is distinct from earlier technologies, but it is by no means as radical a shift in production practice as Bordes suggested. Similarly, work on early Upper Paleolithic sites in and peripheral to Europe suggests the variable emergence of a number of similar technologies marked by a few, often regional or even local, practices (see Brantingham, Kuhn, and Kerry 2004). Indeed, the Middle to Upper Paleolithic transition sometimes shows strong qualitative continuities with a few independent innovations, while in other instances reflecting more complex and substantial production changes. Thus, for the emergence of the Upper Paleolithic from Europe into Eurasia, there was not a single, abrupt ubiquitous change.

In the area of lithic technology, we become aware of many immediate visual and tactile qualities—shape, texture, sharpness, elasticity, and many more. To the extent these qualities become pertinent to the knapper or tool user—or even to the archaeologist—the qualisigns of stone-tool production represent a rich and complex array of actualities. But what an individual knapper relies upon is the recognition of iconic sinsigns, built from subtly appreciated sets of qualisigns. A Peircean sense of this is that an element of fracture or use is an "object of experience." To a knapper engaged in a reduction process, all that is necessary for a sinsign to exist is some visual or tactile pattern significant in the process. Some features, like a "point of impact," "bulbar scar," "bulbar surface," "ripples," or "rays," may become significant at different times, especially when referenced in coordination with other features. When the knapper selects a hard or soft hammer, changes the angle at which material is struck, or affirms some desired result through remembered experience, the process is "wordlessly" semiosic via sinsigns and legisigns.

For the flint knapper, legisigns involve repeated actions and reactions, changeable based on ongoing experience, which move a knapping process toward some desired result. A collection of attributes recognized as always occurring together, becoming in sensory experience a "pattern," relies completely upon iconic or indexical signification *prior to* any codification through some arbitrary symbol, either internal and idiosyncratic or sharable through some system of communication. What may recur independently in two individual knappers as a common experience (rhematic indexical sinsign) directs attention to an object by which its presence is caused. That is, this is a sign that simply points out whatever caused the sign to exist through a very direct associative connection. Peirce's example of this kind of thing, as well as a linguistic example, is that of a spontaneous cry—that is a vocalization with no "content" other than to draw direct attention to the crier, the object of the sign. In the case of a broken piece of rock, the several associated attributes of "conchoidal fracture" comprise a group, always occurring together, that indicate human processes of stone fracture to anyone familiar with stone-tool production. In a less well-known example, we can recognize that the features of rock fracture in certain instances represent particular kinds of impact, angles of contact, qualities of the material being broken, types of hammers, or even individual knappers. What the archaeologist sees are essentially the same indexical signs a knapper uses to control material during reduction, relying on experience and skill to monitor what is going on in the knapping process. Such signs are also a basis of typologies, including those of the archaeologist. To the extent such trait complexes, to use the archaeological term, become routinized in experience (i.e., constitute rhematic indexical legisigns), they fit into the higher elements of the logic of lithic-reduction processes and may be given "symbolic" status by human actors. It should be clear that at the earlier points of hominid evolution, symbolic "naming" of such signs, and even the fuller sinsign/legisign sense of later populations, need not have been extant. But some level of such sign process is present from the earliest stone technology through the advent of language as a communication system and, ultimately, classifications of tools and detritus by variations in knapping practice that are recognized by modern archaeology.

Tied into such constellations of sensed activity, rhematic indexical legisigns may serve the creation of abstractions, which we elaborate upon in Chapter 10, that simplify the appreciation of whole trait complexes when one or more of the associated traits occur. Much of this may happen unconsciously. In lithic analysis, we often read edge wear or other attributes of used tools as indices of function or procedures of production, much in the way individual knappers, though not sharing an explicit explanatory system for how they produce results, may be able to "read" the breakage patterns on each other's tools and detritus (see, for example, Young and Bonnichsen 1984). By comparison, in natural ape sign use, we observe certain foliage modifications that become trail signs among the bonobos (Beckoff 2007, 53–54; Savage-Rumbaugh et al. 1996). The modifications, per se, are merely "breaks" or "trampled" foliage (i.e., iconic legisigns), but they are clear enough to the animals to become actual directive phenomena (i.e., indexical legisigns) insofar as they suggest a concrete direction among two or more possibilities. The suggestion here is that even hominoid cognition is capable of incorporating complex but subtle, though not symbolically elaborated, patterns of observation and response.

Thus, indexical signs may become propositional. A dicent indexical sinsign indicates something about the object it also references. Peirce's example is a weathercock, which is both an object of experience and designated as a sign, and provides information about the sign's object, that is, the wind's direction. Linguistic examples would include various affective cries, which are themselves instances of experience that provide some propositional content about the object, things such as gustatorial cries or nursing cries that are common to humans and the other hominoids. In a lithic example, the shape or length of a flake may provide information about the angle at which a core is struck by a hammerstone, or its potential use in the fabrication of particular tool forms, functioning within a system of continuous alternative outcomes. When such signs become "understood" in process, they are dicent indexical legisigns. Peirce gives the example of what he calls a street cry. Such cries would be exclamations like "hey!" or "oh!"—not grounded in arbitrary convention, but in some non-specific immediacy. Prior to language, "experience" is carried on through natural signs of iconic and indexical form. When such directly experiential signs are in turn recast as rhematic symbols, they may still function as dicent indexical legisigns, as in the cries "Fire!" "Help!" or on a golf course, "Fore!" Each not only draws attention to some object, as with the pronouns "this" and "that," but also provides some specific content about the world, so the sign as a dicent is not merely a sign of possibility, but one of actual existence. Understanding these rhematic signs as serving propositional interests helps us see why such speech acts as crying "Fire!" in a crowded theater are often treated differently from other speech acts—they are different semiosically. This brings us to some observations about immediate experience and early language as it relates to stone technology.

Within the process of stone-tool production, we should note that any recognizable pattern may become associated with a vocalization (whether symbolic or affective). In that way, the earliest "words" would mainly have carried indexical information, drawing attention as indexical rhemes to some phenomenon present in the moment that conformed to a common pattern in the process. Thus, rhematic symbols can connect an object to a general concept grounded in indices of visual appearance or process. Rhematic symbols have not been observed in the wild among hominoid apes, though the great apes have clearly demonstrated the capacity to learn and use such symbols in experimental contexts. In ape language experiments, the level of propositions, or dicent symbols, involve such manual displays as "give hat" or "like drink," though the sense of the dicent might as easily be carried by the rhemes "hat" or "drink" in context, or by a comparable indexical gesture. Such usage is observed in human infants who are starting to use speech. These observations echo correspondence theory of truth in the works of various modern philosophers, though it should be clear from our discussion that language involves more than simple correspondence to the world.

All of these sign types are incipient in early hominid behavior as reflected by stone technology. What humans evolved as a capacity, and what archaeologists apply as analysis and interpretation, constitute "the symbolic argument" of Peirce's classification. An argument builds upon premises (which are themselves dicent symbols) to the construction of conclusions and truth systems. These can take several different forms, including the logical principles of deduction, induction, or abduction. Arguments can also take such forms as mathematical formulae, narrative plot, poetry, or myth structure. The argument in particular and symbols in general are clearly very important types of signs in human semiosis. However, they are not the only types of signs we use, nor even the most important sign types for us. As we have seen, dicent indexical legisigns and dicent sinsigns are powerful sign types for us as well—and it is perhaps no coincidence that these are crucially important in semiosis of the diverse ape species. To be clear, however, to the extent that our capacity for the argument has any connection to the world, it is built atop simpler iconic and indexical signs working independently, and without cognitive instantiation as symbols. Our symbols work in the service of iconicity and indexicality, sign capacities that are central to our actual sensory experience. In other terms, "the symbolic argument" is a gloss for higher functions of logic and narrative construction grounded in the underpinnings of more specific types of signs in our repertoire.

Artifacts have always been taken as "signs" by the archaeologists, but they have not always been formally recognized as having a ground in the myriad of signs in the ongoing behavior stream of past cultures. Most archaeologists would claim that they do not have access to the minds of pre-literate people, much less pre-linguistic apes, but this is only partly true. That is, much of the behavioral process underlying tool production is *guided* and regulated by the apprehension of many of the same qualisigns, sinsigns, and legisigns that the archaeologist sees. Indeed, attention to the Peircean categories can help us construct arguments about the cognitive capacities of the hominids who made tools, whether fully *Homo sapiens* or some earlier and less cognitively derived member of the Hominidae. And in many respects we may also compare the capacities of humans directly to the great apes and other anthropoids by fully recognizing the levels of sign activity in any particular behavior or material "object."

What can we say about the mental processes underlying some specific material artifact? And can we extend from some of those processes to associated capacities of communication or language? With the iconic legisign, we essentially have a general type, each token of which is further an index of the process through which it originated. In archaeological terms, the iconic legisign is a sort of simple "mental template." In the context of lithic studies, a bulbar scar, microwear, secondary flaking, reduction sequences, and so on are much more likely to function as explicit signs for the archaeologist or paleoanthropologist, but are at least nascent for the tool-using creature as well.

Because these capacities are shared widely within the higher primates whose cognitive repertoires do not include language, none of our observations about iconicity or indexicality necessarily suggest the presence of "language" (that is to say, habitual symbolling) in a fossil species (see Sebeok 1992 for the groundwork of zoosemiotics). With ape language experiments, we find great apes using manual signs as rhematic symbols, but we do not see rhematic symbol use in the wild. Inasmuch as ape language experiments show the capacity among bonobos, chimpanzees, gorillas, and orangutans to employ symbolic rhemes in association with propositional behavior, what would we expect the material associations of language to be in an early hominid? The answer to this question is essentially that with increases in cranial capacity we should expect complex multistage processes that we can read as solidifying into locally diverse but distinctive patterns. As shared experience emerges among those wielding a particular technology, the conventional nature of symbols tends to produce increasingly consistent outcomes. This is what we observe among contemporary knappers; that is, individuals develop different lexicon for discussion of what they do. In isolation, there would not be ample opportunity for the symbolic system to dominate the emphasis in complex multistage processes. So, the archaeological question becomes, how "shared" are knapping processes in either experience or potential symbolic reference?

When a basic tool form comes into use, as it does in limited ways with the Acheulian tools of Homo erectus and much more systematically with the Mousterian tools of Neanderthals, we may project the potential existence of rhematic symbols. The case is much stronger where there occur in the record variations of forms devoted to similar functions. The archaeological record described by contributors to "Early Human Behaviour in Global Context" (Petraglia and Korisettar 1998) and "The Early Upper Paleolithic beyond Western Europe" (Brantingham, Kuhn, and Kerry 2004) manifests the slow expansion of stylistic variations that takes off during the later Upper Paleolithic. Steven Kuhn's (1995; see also Cunliffe 1994) work on the Middle Paleolithic details some of the production processes in terms of linear decision-making models and other complexities. If we attend closely to the practices Kuhn describes, "Neanderthals" or populations employing the Mousterian technology seem to have been using dicent symbols, as manifest by the complexity of the production process for the assemblage of multiple tool types and their ubiquity in the assemblages. In effect, each tool "type" of the kind Bordes asserted in the Mousterian is a "rhematic iconic legisign," which could easily be referenced by an arbitrary symbol. At the least, each tool form is also a "rhematic indexical legisign" referencing its function in the practice of the tool maker, as well as in the eye of the archaeologist. Presuming that form and function are working closely together in the tool kit, then the propositional potential of the association seems likely. We know there is limited use of dicent symbols by apes in manual sign experiments, but where the ape appears not to employ dicent symbols in the wild, we may infer from the complexity and pattern of the lithic assemblages that the Archaic *Homo sapiens* were labeling at least some of their forms and processes.

With increasing diversity in the technological system, including longer sequences of production necessary for the creation of a single tool form, we should expect parallel development of propositional forms into potential "arguments" shared among knappers—the use of symbolic rhemes to negotiate logical fields, compare work, or instruct. At such a point, the "symbol" begins to tag the experience of the animal, conditioning what is "seen" or "experienced" within an arbitrary but locally shared system of labels for behavior. We have argued elsewhere (see especially Haworth 2006 and Chapter 11 in this volume), the "capacity" for full-blown human language at its inception would not have necessarily generated "speech behaviors" mirroring every aspect of life. And isolation of groups would assure that diverse elements of the behavior stream, working in different environments, would create ample material variation to be accommodated in a developing symbolic system of common signs. The "empirical" process of living, even with very similar material conditions, does not guarantee identical outcomes in the symbolic realm.

TOOLS, POPULATIONS, AND EVOLUTION

The Peircean classification applied in material/behavioral analysis can help us recognize exactly how overlapping and dynamic are the processes in Anthropoid semiosis. We see these processes not as static arrangements of sign types, but rather as a flow from qualisigns up through the potentialities of sense, perceived rhematic possibilities, and then actualities in sense-perception (Figure 9.2). Our human experience may have a symbolic emphasis, but much of the actual experience is carried on iconically and enriched or coordinated indexically. We are, as we constantly like to stress, historically visual thinkers. Our symbols serve much more fundamental sign functions, making unlimited human semiosis a truly magnificent "*innenwelt*" of patterns and processes—a "covering" atop experience that conditions our sense of the world.

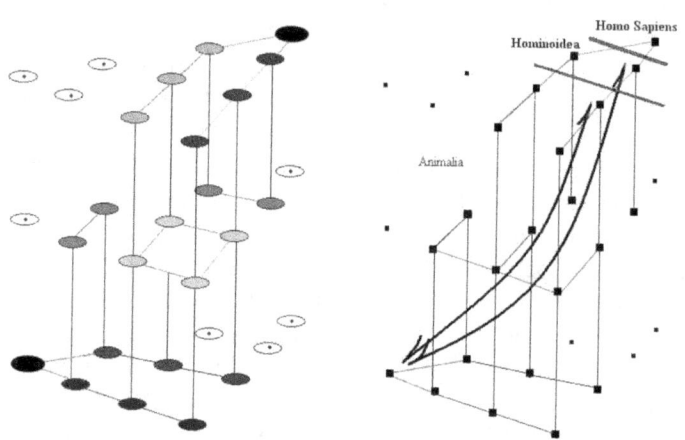

Figure 9.2. The Peircean Sign-Field as a Process Model. *Source:* T. Prewitt.

Given current evidence, the "argument" is a sign type unique to human semiosis, though symbols are shared with other species and most of the sign field is shared widely among animals. We do encounter some evidence with stone-tool use of the "argument" in the logic of concatenated patterns and forms, especially in protracted lithic-reduction routines (and many other areas of the material record) involving complex decision making, but this is something in direct experience we only encounter with our own species, *Homo sapiens sapiens*. In semiotic terms, we may conclude that: *It is not the symbol, but the argument that most clearly differentiates us from other hominids and hominoids.*

To repeat what bears repeating, the great apes are capable in laboratory settings of rhematic symbol use, and even simple dicent symbol use. They do not seem to engage in this sort of semiosis in the wild, however, or at least have not been observed to do so. They possess the necessary capacity for symbol use, but it appears that they must be taught in order to bring the ability into even basic fruition. It now is quite clear that they do not possess the ability for the construction of arguments and symbolic world systems, things that are an inherent aspect of extant human semiosis.

No doubt, some members of the genus Homo other than ourselves did use symbols. With *Homo erectus* we see evidence for rhematic symbols (in regularized tool forms) and possibly a nascent ability for dicent symbols, and with Neanderthals, rhematic and dicent symbols were apparently used habitually, as evidenced by the allocation of tool functions to specific forms. In neither case, do we see any *necessary* evidence for the argument. Even after Neanderthals were clearly in limited interaction with *Homo sapiens sapiens*, having acquired or paralleled some Upper Paleolithic tools of the earliest Sapiens, it is still uncertain whether they were capable of adopting the complex lithic-reduction complexes of our species. And without evidence of substantial "displacement" in the use of symbols, there can be little basis for presuming any of the more complex forms of logical construction than "naming" and very basic "predication." Based on current evidence, humans remain alone in constructing logical worlds and truth systems.

Even though "the argument" is what differentiates humans from other Hominoidea, it is not clear that our own species has always used the argument in full-blown language as we know it. Just as chimps and bonobos have the capacity for symbol use but do not actually engage in it without being taught, humans may have had the latent capacity for argumentation early on without the ability being widely manifest. That is, a full capacity for human logic may have developed gradually through the enrichment of the use of rhematic and dicent symbols, without "language" per se at the beginning, but evolving into language as we know it (Haworth 2007; see also Haworth and Prewitt 2010). As more and more evidence from the crucial period becomes available (c. fifty to two hundred thousand years ago), we should be able to further refine our view of these issues. But what is clear, as we point out in other chapters, archaeological evidence for the argument in the form of narrative and visual abstraction does not occur until relatively late in the record, as recently as about fifteen thousand years ago. At the least, we must develop a case for the sort of tool evidence that would indicate an earlier presence of the "logical argument" in Paleolithic populations and differentiate that capacity clearly from more foundational sign capacities.

NOTES

1. Within this discussion, I have provided general references to Peirce (i.1861–1909) through the Collected Papers (ed. Hartshorn and Weiss 1931–1935, and Burks 1958), and to de Saussure (i.1906–1911) through the Course in General Linguistics (ed. Bally and Sechehaye 1915 [1959]).

2. The object/representamen relation is somewhat similar to the idea of paradigmatic meaning in the work of de Saussure, though it takes a more classificatory approach to potential meaning, rather than a view from immediate context.

3. The interpretant is somewhat similar to the idea of syntagmatic meaning in the work of de Saussure.

WORKS CITED

Beckoff, Marc. 2007. *Animals Matter*. Boston: Shambhala Publications.

Brantingham, P. Jeffrey, Steven L. Kuhn, and Kristopher W. Kerry, eds. 2004. *The Early Upper Paleolithic beyond Western Europe*. Berkeley: University of California Press.

Cunliffe, Barry. 1994. *The Oxford Illustrated Prehistory of Europe*. Oxford: Oxford University Press.

Deely, John. 1982. *Introducing Semiotic: Its History and Doctrine*. Bloomington: Indiana University Press.

———. 1994. *The Human Use of Signs or Elements of Anthroposemiosis*. Lanham, MD: Rowman & Littlefield.

Haworth, Karen A. 2006. "Upper Paleolithic Art, Autism, and Cognitive Style: Implications for the Evolution of Language." *Semiotica* 162: 1/4, 127–74.

———. 2007. "Cognitive Style and Zoosemiotics." In *Semiotics 2004/2005*, edited by Stacy Monahan, Ben Smith, and Terry Prewitt. Ottawa: Legas Press

Haworth, Karen A., and Terry J. Prewitt. 2010. "Two Steps toward Semiotic Capacity: Out of the Muddy Concept of Language." *Semiotica* 178: 1/4, 53–79.

Kuhn, Steven. 1995. *Mousterian Lithic Technology*. Princeton, NJ: Princeton University Press.

Merrell, Floyd. 2007. "Why I Believe Becoming Peircean Is Preferable." In *Signs*, Vol. 1, 1–28.

Parmentier, Richard J. 1994. *Signs in Society: Studies in Semiotic Anthropology*. Bloomington: Indiana University Press.

Peirce, Charles Sanders. i.1861–1909. The abbreviation CP followed by volume number(s) separated from paragraph number(s) by a period, is to the eight-volume *Collected Papers of Charles Sanders Peirce,* Vols. I–IV, edited by Charles Hartshorne and Paul Weiss. Cambridge, MA: Harvard University Press, 1931–1935; Vols. VII and VIII, edited by Arthur W. Burks. Cambridge, MA: Harvard University Press, 1958. CP references are chronologized principally on the basis of the "Bibliography" provided by Arthur W. Burks in CP 8, pp. 249–330.

Petraglia, Michael D., and Ravi Korisettar, eds. 1998. *Early Human Behaviour in Global Context: The Rise and Diversity of the Lower Paleolithic Record*. New York: Routledge.

de Saussure, Ferdinand. i.1906–1911. *Course in General Linguistics*. Edited by Charles Bally and Albert Sechehaye, prepared from auditors' notes (Geneva, 1915); translated from French by Wade Baskin. New York: The Philosophical Library (1959).

Savage-Rumbaugh, E. Sue, Shelley L. Williams, Takeshi Furuichi, and Kano Takayoshi.1996. "Language Perceived: *Paniscus* Branches Out." In *Great Ape Societies*, edited by William C. McGrew, Linda F. Marchant, and Toshisada Nishida, 173–85. Cambridge: Cambridge University Press.

Sebeok, Thomas A. 1992. "Zoosemiotic Components of Human Communication." In *Introducing Semiotics: An Anthology of Readings*, edited by M. Danesi and D. Santeramo, 153–84. Toronto: Canadian Scholar's Press.

Spinks, C. W. 1991. *Peirce and Triadomania: A Walk in the Semiotic Wilderness.* New York: Mouton de Gruyter.

Young, David E., and Robson Bonnichsen. 1984. *Understanding Stone Tools: A Cognitive Approach*. Peopling of the Americas Process Series: Vol. 1. Center for the Study of Early Man. University of Maine at Orono.

Chapter Ten

The Bubble Analogy

Karen's Story: The previous chapter presents a groundwork for semiotically assessing the transformation of our species through the analysis of lithic remains of Paleolithic populations. However, for my own purposes, I found it helpful to develop a means of envisioning the overall changes in cognition from the perspective of individual animals. For this I used an analogy, one of an expanding bubble, as a simple reference to the expanding brain of the primate lineage. If we assume the basic point that the visual/holistic form of cognition is the fundamental aspect of thought for most species, then an individual's sensory and memory universe can be seen as a set of specific perceptions contained as a bounded array within a particular place and time, a bubble of experience. When we recognize that the primary trait of hominid evolution centers on the expansion of the brain, then we can look at the transformation through time to be an expansion of the boundaries defining that perceptual worldview. I used this process of expanding holistic experience to present an argument for the eventual transformation to dominant analytical thought.

I found this analogy helpful when presenting my ideas on human evolution to students. I would begin with a favorite observation that when it comes to understanding the mechanics of the evolution of human intelligence, size isn't everything. As we have noted before, the paleontological record establishes a zenith for the size for the hominid brain during the time of the Neanderthals. Yet, the archaeological record does not evince modern human behavior until the Mesolithic and Neolithic, and by that time the average cranial capacity of our species had become well established at about thirteen hundred cubic centimeters.

In this chapter we present a thought experiment to elucidate the internal cognitive transformations that we believe must have taken place in this evolution of human brain functions. We call the experiment "the bubble analogy." A first step for developing the bubble analogy must involve establishing some background on the thought processes of other species. This can be accomplished by looking again at the sign categories discussed in the previous chapter. The hierarchical nature of the distinctions stressed in the illustrations were meant to highlight an aspect of Peirce's works that is generally understood in the community of semiotic scholars but is emphasized here for its utility in drawing distinctions between species and in cognitive developments through time.

As we have mentioned before, the base-level category of the qualisign involves distinguishing difference within one's environment that is a necessary aspect of any living creature, within the sensory capacity of any species. Through this lens, there are whole areas of study in semiotics that look at interactions within plant species, giving rise to the areas of biosemiotics and even phytosemiotics. The term zoosemiotics has been established to reference signification within the cognitive realms of *all* animals. As has been amply demonstrated by animal behavior studies, signification in zoosemiosis can sometimes be represented even at the levels of rhematic and dicent symbols. There are numerous examples that can be cited here, but at the very least one should reference the works of Wolfgang Köhler (1925, 1947), Thomas Sebeok (1972, 1974, 1980, 1981), John C. Lilly (1975), Jane Goodall (1986), Dian Fossey (1983), Roger Fouts (1997), Sue Savage-Rumbaugh (1998), and Temple Grandin (1995, 2005).

The compliment of signing capacities specific to humans is designated anthroposemiosis (Sebeok 1974). While the term anthroposemiosis is an ungainly one, it serves well to conveniently distinguish humanity's specific semiosic world experience (with a strong tendency toward *semiotic* rendering of experience through symbols). For our use, we see the zoosemiosic and anthroposemiosic distinctions as roughly differentiating those forms of cognition dominated by the visual/holistic mode on the one hand, and the particular cognitive world of modern *Homo sapiens,* which is more dominated by the analytic mode. The dominating analytic mode builds proposition onto proposition comprising Peirce's ultimate sign category, "the argument." Unfortunately, as discussed in Chapter 2 of this volume, one also encounters in works by other scholars the use of the word "language" to distinguish this specialized capacity of humans. This is why we make a distinction between language as a modeling system and language as a communication system. The confusing usage came about over the last century in the general and long-standing primate language debate. As studies continued to demonstrate unforeseen capabilities within other species and delved into the rather simplistic existing definitions for the word "language," those seeking to continue to underline our cognitive distinctions, rather than embracing similarities, chose to change and *restrict* the definition for the term "language" until it no longer bore a reliable meaning. Common usage, moreover, now only serves to muddy the waters of the debate in general, since "language" is often applied to any kind of animal communication (see Haworth and Prewitt 2006, 2010).

We would also like to point out that within the zoosemiosic realm are other equally distinctive cognitive manifestations that define each species and which vary by differences in perceptual architecture, as well as brain structure and chemistry. Along with anthroposemiosis, we need to recognize that there are differences between pongid semiosis, gorilla semiosis, cetacean semiosis, canine semiosis, equine semiosis, and so on. Any discussion on the generalities of intelligence and communicative capabilities among species should proceed via a fuller understanding of the variation that occurs for each species-specific evolutionary journey.

While recognizing the varying specifics of cognition in animal species, for our purposes here the general trend to the holistic mode still stands. Although animal behavior studies do work to demonstrate capabilities more in keeping with human thought, they fall short of providing a thorough understanding of the mind/cognitive universe of others. This is because intelligence studies in general take on the task through a classically analytical method by dissecting human thought processes into types, then making comparisons to observed behavior in other species. This is necessarily an unwieldy process, particularly when dealing with non-primate species, whose intellectual evolutionary journey must have taken quite different roads. Still, the comparisons are all we have to work with within the existing academic canon. Volume upon volume presents new ways to subdivide and categorize human thought and somehow map those types onto other species. Some examples of these segmentations include Dale Jamieson's (2002) content ascription and hyperintensionality; or Ann Russon's and David Begun's (2004) symbolic constructions, cognitive hierarchization, generativity, metarepresentation, self-concept, imitation, deception, logico-mathematical reasoning, and fluidity of thought; or Jesse Bering's and Daniel Povinelli's (2003) intentionality, imitation, goal-directed tasking and reinterpretation; or Francesco Antinucci's (1989, 3-9) sensory motor intelligence, classification, and seriation.

Rarely within these categorizations have there been attempts made to place types into hierarchies or arrays that might signal a progression through time. Instead, there is only searching for the instances of "like-thinking" encountered in other species to provide the assumed evolutionary ascent, looking at the relative evolutionary distance in the species, we presume, to provide some form of developing cognitive system.

One obvious exception to this process of segmentation without hierarchy lies in Jean Piaget's stages of development (Antinucci 1989, 11-17), which were derived from observations of human cognition as it progresses in the ontogenic process. Given the assumptions behind the axiom that ontogeny recapitulates phylogeny, Piaget's levels could prove very useful in conceptualizing the evolutionary steps to human intelligence (human semiosis). This is exactly what was attempted in Antinucci's edited volume *Cognitive Structure and Development in Nonhuman Primates* (1989). But the work instead determined that such a recapitulation across species does not, in fact, exist. Antinucci concludes (251) that "the evolutionary path leading to the structuring of human cognitive capacities . . . seems to have taken several independent 'turns' at various steps of its long course."

These forms of analysis of intelligence across the animal kingdom are actually inherently speciesist (if we may apply that term) in that the typologies are derived from the human repertoire without first recognizing the differing capabilities of other genera. Working with the human example as a starting point is a problem we recognized years ago in evaluating the various ape language experiments of the last century. While this work provided the impetus recognizing hitherto unexpected mental acuity in other species, each example always fell short of providing real insight into the nature of their extant communication systems. We were requiring the subject animals to generate the translation to our system, rather than simply seeking to understand their natural modes of interaction and exchange.

Such segmentation of human cognition, then, doesn't really further the search for continuity between species and necessarily leaves us in the dark with regard to the specific cognitive faculties of other animals. Without this basic understanding, we are left with confusion and even awe when encountering certain aspects of cognition that do not readily fit in with the norms of standard analytic capabilities of humans. We seek out the forms of cognition where humans excel and ignore areas of our weakness. Hence, we have the constant source of news media materials on the oddity of animal cognitive achievements or even of the so-called savant achievements of some humans. Examples of such reports can be found in Walker (2009), Morton and Page (1992), Treffert and Wallace (2002), Heaton and Wallace (2004), and Howe (1989), or for more immediately accessible examples, see the online site Newser's "Animal Intelligence" page.

True understanding of evolutionary development then, from our perspective, should proceed from the initial step of describing the perceived world of the holistic mind. Understanding this form of cognition is vital to understanding the several aspects of progression toward analytic thought. For this approach, we return to the examples provided by those holistic thinkers we introduced before. Below are a few astute self-analytical observations provided in autobiographical works by Grandin (1995, 2005) and Prince-Hughes (2004), which present a mind, or visual thinker as Temple Grandin terms it, where there apparently is an almost one-to-one correspondence between sensations perceived from the external reality. Memory in the visual mode consists of almost purely iconic representations—the map constitutes a *virtual* territory. Seen as a whole, the map envelopes an entire tableau of perceptions as an event in time. The mental representation is not simply a static snapshot or photographic visual image, but also includes impressions of sound, smell, touch, and any other sensory experience of a particular event in ostensibly complete fashion. The exceptional memories of high-holistic individuals, however, are very distinct wholes that are not easily partitioned. Specific aspects of one memory do not easily relate to segments of other memories, so generalized concepts are built out of a collection of very specific past examples. For instance, Grandin (2005, 261) notes that the word "bowl" calls to mind a large file of images of very specific bowls of past experience rather than a conglomeration of characteristics that might signify "bowlness." All in all, a holistic form of modeling the world is a very direct one that provides more of a living-in-the-moment experience of life. As Grandin (2005, 65) puts it, "Normal people see and hear schemas, not raw sensory data."

Grandin describes her visualizations as akin to video recordings that can be played back over and over. We should consider again how she describes her design process in her book *Thinking in Pictures: My Life with Autism* (1995, 21):

> My imagination works like the computer graphics programs that created the lifelike dinosaurs in *Jurassic Park*. When I do an equipment simulation in my imagination or work on an engineering problem, it is like seeing it on a videotape in my mind. I can view it from any angle, placing myself above or below the equipment and rotating it at the same time. I don't need a fancy graphics program that can produce three-dimensional design simulations. I can do it better and faster in my head.

Prince-Hughes uses a surprisingly similar analogy to describe her recall of a childhood memory (2004, 16):

> When I close my eyes, I can play it back like a three-dimensional tape, replete with smells, the sensations, and my feelings about it. I have always had this photographic or eidetic memory, and all of my many recollections of the past have a quality that makes them seem almost more real than the present.

Grandin (2005) also speaks of visual memory working even in situations that normally involve abstract thinking, such as the recall of a conversation (10):

> We were sitting there talking, and he started asking really personal questions. I don't remember what they were, because I almost never remember specific

words and sentences from conversations. That's because autistic people think in pictures; we have almost no words running through our heads at all. Just a stream of images. So I don't remember the verbal details of the questions; I just remember that he asked them.

Working with the high level of detail stored in these kinds of memories can be in some way limiting and presents some memory problems in itself. Because visual thinkers must take in everything and cannot easily filter out irrelevant aspects of an environment, their understanding of complex situations is derived only through long-term contact. Grandin in her book *Animals in Translation* (2005) speaks of the time it took to gain an understanding of the overall functioning of all of the components of a meatpacking plant where she was doing consulting work (253):

> One disadvantage of my type of thinking that I probably share with animals is that it takes a long time to download enough details to learn a complex sequence. To do it, I have to create a computer video in my imagination. With the plant, all told, it took six months to download a complete videotape of the entire place into my head. Twenty-four Tuesday afternoons.

As stated previously, the holistic cognitive style seems to be a point of commonality between humans and other animal species. And this idea is supported by Grandin and Prince-Hughes, where connection to other species is a recurring theme (see Grandin's *Animals in Translation: Using the Mysteries of Autism to Decode Animal Behavior* and Prince-Hughes' *Gorillas among Us: A Primate Ethnographer's Book of Days*). Grandin just comes right out and proclaims (2005, 6–8):

> Autistic people can think the way animals think. Of course, we also think the way people think—we aren't *that* different from normal humans. Autism is a kind of way station on the road from animals to humans, which puts autistic people like me in a perfect position to translate "animal talk" into English. I can tell people why their animals are doing the things they do.
> Animals are like autistic savants. In fact, I'd go so far as to say that animals might actually *be* autistic savants. Animals have special talents normal people don't, the same way autistic people have special talents normal people don't; and at least some animals have special forms of genius normal people don't, the same way autistic savants have special forms of genius. I think most of the time animal genius probably happens for the same reason autistic genius does: a difference in the brain autistic people share with animals.

At the very least, autistic people feel a very great affinity to other mammals, and that is the prevailing impetus behind Prince-Hughes' decision to work in primate ethology. In her volume *Songs of the Gorilla Nation* (2004), she describes her initial reaction to observing the gorilla enclosure at her very first visit to a zoo (93):

> I cracked my eyes open, and through windows of glass and mist I saw them. Black and solid and timeless against the running and changing wet sat gorillas. Through the rain and a lifetime of waiting, they did not look at me, but they knew I was there. I sat still. I sat still. I sat for an hour, two, and three. I sat still.
>
> They didn't look at one another, and they didn't look at me. Instead, they looked at *everything*. They were so subtle and steady that I felt like I was watching people for the first time in my whole life, really watching them, free from acting, free from the oppression that comes with brash and bold sound, the blinding stares and uncomfortable closeness that mark the talk of human people. In contrast, these captive people spoke softly, their bodies poetic, their faces and dance poetic, spinning conversations out of the moisture and perfume, out of the ground and out of the past. They were like me.
>
> They didn't have to narrow their vision and cut the world apart. To look closely would have kept them from seeing and choked off the moving and breathing parts of the world, making it flat—worth little.

If we assume a holistic worldview for other species and see this reality more clearly through the descriptions of the human visual thinkers, we can then begin to have some real understanding behind what is now seen as enigmatic abilities for mapping territories, group recognition, and many other awe-inspiring capabilities we observe in other animals. This begins to explain the prodigious and uncanny feats of memory exhibited by human savants.

With these descriptions of the visual thinker in mind, it is clear why the thought bubble presented itself as a means of illustration. Picture in your mind a circle as an illustration of the holistic memory of a particular place, event, or object; then consider the circle as colored in vivid hues, representing the level of detail captured in the mind of a primarily visual thinker. This representation seems to reflect what Merlin Donald (1991) terms "episodic memory." Donald's tripartite model for the development of human consciousness recognizes a necessary stage in which our cognitive capabilities were limited by a time construct (149–53). The memory base, then, would be like a conglomeration of bubbles, distinct from each other and largely separate from each other, like marbles in a jar.

The bubble can illustrate the evolutionary trend by imagining the size of the bubble as representing the extent of data a particular animal is capable of processing at any given time. Consider the situation presented in Rivas and Burghardt's article on anthropomorphism (2002, 15) where mice released into a field could easily return to their forested habitat twenty meters away but were unable to orient toward the habitat when released thirty meters distant. With the enlargement of the neocortex in the various mammalian species, then there would be a resultant increase in the size of that mental world—so the bubble expands. Note, however, that increases in cortex size are formed by geometric additions of off-the-shelf neurons, but this results in an *exponential* increase in the number of synaptic interconnections between those neurons. The bubble expansion is not a simple, directly proportional increase.

At this point, we need to reiterate the way analytical aspects of thought function within the holistic realm. In order for any problem-solving activity to occur, there need to be certain aspects of perception within the thought bubbles that are brought into notice and relations made between them. However, these relations would be limited by the amount of data housed within the bubble. For example, consider the problem-solving experiments noted in Köhler's *The Mentality of Apes* (1925, 12–16). He contrasts the behavior of dogs and chickens when presented with the problem of food placed behind an L-shaped mesh barrier. The dog moves quickly around the barrier, while the hens simply move about in zigzag fashion along the front wall of the barrier at a point closest to the food on the other side. The perceptual field is obviously greater with the dog and, hence, provides an enhanced relational process.

In terms of our bubble analogy, if the full-color bubble represents the holistic style, we must now model the analytic mode within these bubbles to illustrate the problem-solving aspect of thought demonstrated by all species in some form or another. Analytic processing alters perceptions and sense information in several ways. Rather than storing a more directly iconic representation, the sensory input is broken down and organized into salient characteristics. In this model, the imaginary bubble presents some separated content within the vivid color representation of the whole. Certain elements of the environment are considered more worthy of note, depicted as nodes of relevant data and represented by the most salient characteristics, and are thus schematized around only the important aspects of sensation, for example, the redness of ripe fruit or protective aspect of the tall tree or rock crevasse.

This is an essential element in the creation of rhemes, arbitrary signs that cue memory to a constellation of stored perceptions in the form of indexical or iconic sinsigns and legisigns. This segmentation allows, then, a second tier of data manipulation—a process of interconnecting nodes within memory, which results in the construction of generalized concepts and logical types. These concepts are then abstracted in a codified manner, what we consider to be a kind of mental shorthand. The noted aspects of the environment provide needed data for survival. It is how an animal determines food sources, danger, and shelter. Within our full-color bubble, then, are schematized figures with interconnecting lines that show correlation of some sort.

This process of abstraction becomes the ideation behind the stick figure drawings of children and the stylized artwork of human culture (Haworth

2006). Unlike high-holistic savant artists, people in general tend to draw what we *know*, not what we *see* (Selfe 1977, 98). We use the word "shorthand" here in referencing these abstractions to specifically highlight the efficiency that this mode of thought must engender. Cognitive typologies, then, become the *natural* method used by the analytic thinkers of academia to segment the cognitive process in the effort to understand it. In this sense elements of the environment are "seen" through their defining characteristics. This becomes an automatic and unconscious activity that is also influenced by cultural norms, hence the word "house" for most English speakers often invokes the mental image of a square (walls and floor) topped by a triangle roof with added rectangles for windows and doors, even including the chimney complete with the puff of smoke, though that reality has not been a norm for generations.

The importance of making connections was recognized by William Golding years ago in his fictional work, *The Inheritors* (1955, 194):

> Lok discovered "Like." He had used likeness all this life without being aware of it. Fungi on a tree were ears, the word was the same but acquired a distinction by circumstances that could never apply to the sensitive things on the side of his head. Now, in a convulsion of the understanding Lok found himself using likeness as a tool as surely as ever he had used a stone to hack at sticks or meat. Likeness could grasp the white-faced hunters with a hand, could put them into the world where they were thinkable and not a random and unrelated irruption.

Golding's character here is presumably a Neanderthal seeking to understand the mysterious powers of the archaic *Homo sapiens* who had invaded his territory. The story is, of course, based on early, but now greatly revised, notions of the *Homo* subspecies. However, it is interesting to note how Golding intuitively arrived at what turns out to be a significant aspect of evolutionary change.

HOMINID SEMIOSIS

Now imagine the eventual progression of change resulting from the continued enlargement of the brain in primates as manifest among hominids. With the exponential increase in the mental world, the attendant analytical capabilities can be seen as multiplying to an extent that they produce significant new behaviors—greater and greater problem-solving attention within the general field of experience. Enhanced problem solving would increase the extent to which the focused behaviors conferred selective advantages, which in turn would produce ever-greater capacities for analytic thought across generations.

Again, turning to our full-color bubble metaphor, the space may now be thought of as variously imbued with connections between certain nodes in the perceptual landscape, while definition of the circle can be less clearly defined. In a graphic representation, the circle representing the consciousness bubble would be better indicated by a dashed line, rather than a solid one. Up to this point the elements of analytical thinking so far provided in our model occur within the single holistic bubble of an episodic memory—a unit confined by either time or place. The elements must exist within the framework for a primarily holistic thinker (human or otherwise), as connections are necessary to any level of problem-solving capability. This, we think, is crucial to understanding the behaviors we observe in ethological studies. The analytical aspects of thought, then, evident in other primates and the early *Homo* species are *mostly* confined to particular episodes of memory, and analytical thought is *for the most part* limited to a particular bubble of immediate experience. However impressive the communicative behaviors we might note in other species, there is always a point at which the comparison to modern humans pales, and this limitation we consider to be an episodic limitation. The rock used to crack open a hard fruit is recognized to be useful for other feeding sessions and is retained and reused, but that is not necessarily shared directly between individuals.

Returning to comparison with non-human species, the primary point we set up with the bubble analogy is that aspects of analytical thinking exist, though to a lesser degree, for most species. The *relational* ideas about various extracted elements in one's surroundings provide the creative, inventive, and general problem-solving behaviors we find in most species in one form or another, but typically operating only on the iconic and indexical level. We suggest that the memory of the holistic thinker might be illustrated as a series of bubbles, wherein the entire set of perceptual data for individual events is represented in full-color tones, as the detail of recall is extensive and relatively complete. Within these bubbles certain elements can be seen as relational to other elements and indicated by highlighted points connected by lines and representing aspects of analytical cognition within the holistic gestalt experience. But, in non-human semiosis those relations remain for the most part attached to the single experience essentially through iconic or indexical sinsigns and legisigns, the precise limitation on analytic thinking Donald noted as "episodic memory" (1991, 149–53).

Now, consider that the continued gross expansion of the brain creates elaborations of the neural connections through synapses, allowing for an ever-increasing facility with "bubble logic" and an ability to make metaphorical connections. We envision in the Upper Paleolithic individuals who not only take features within their immediate environment for use in obtaining their needs, but begin to make alterations to the environment in order to enhance their utility. Such refinements in the ability to alter surrounding conditions, of course, would provide impetus for continued neurological changes. In our analogy, then, at some point the bubble of color imagery and interconnected nodes would serve a mind with analytical capabilities that come into balance with the holistic, where interconnections sometimes occur between bubbles that are lined up in cause-and-effect fashion, in a *sequenced* arrangement amid the overall conglomeration of experiences. Such alignments would enhance the propositional or dicent quality of the semiosis, as in the elaboration of forms and functions evinced in the prominent stylistic variations of the late Upper Paleolithic.

At this point in the long history of physiological transformations in brain size for the hominid line, an upper limit on the evolutionary trend was reached, though the benefits of the analytical mode continued to press for enhancement. Here, then, occurs the final alteration of perceptual data in analytical thinking—the move from "dicent symbols" toward the Peircean "argument." The brain's internal architecture needed further change, and internal structure began to replace the detail of perceptual memory with the shorthand of the schematized elements necessary for interconnection. For our analogy, the full-color bubble would be replaced with, say, a half-tone one, and the connecting nodes now occur across the episodic bubbles, which have lost their clear definition and meld together as abstracted lines of events in a series. The analytical mode has begun to dominate cognition. Where before there were networks of nodes within a single bubble, there are now networks between bubbles. *Homo sapiens* begins to play with cognitive building blocks. We'll let your imagination take you wherever that might lead.[1]

The Upper Paleolithic record attests to cognitive developments far beyond anything produced by earlier populations; it represents a time of invention. In the chapter on the Upper Paleolithic in Barry Cunliffe's volume *Prehistory of Europe* (1994), Paul Mellars (42–78) declares the era "revolutionary." Of stone-tool technology he notes a "proliferation" of blade forms. He continues, noting "significant shifts in stone tool production can be seen in the much greater dynamism and innovation shown by Upper Paleolithic communities in creating a much wider and more diverse *range* of tool forms than those produced during earlier periods" (46). Mellars goes on to note that an even greater level of creativity and innovation is evident in bone- and antler-tool technologies (51). The Upper Paleolithic aesthetic creativity also stems from the very earliest communities with a proliferation of carvings and decorative ornamentation, in addition to the famous cave paintings of southern France and northern Spain (51–52). Societal transformations are an equally important part of the Upper Paleolithic revolution, with the first indications of large settlement activity, group stylistic and technical variations, and emergent trading and exchange networks (59–67).

Our surmised neural transformations for the advent of the increase in analytical function appears to be demonstrated by perspectives in cognitive neuroscience, including the work of one of the leading researchers in the field. Michael Gazzaniga, in his volume *Human: The Science Behind What Makes Us Unique* (2008), notes genetics research that indicates genes related to the development of the human brain have undergone mutation at least twice in recent times, relatively speaking (16). The change represented by one of these mutations involved alterations in neural networking of the left hemisphere of the neocortex (27–32), which we see as a means of enhancing the analytic mode. But, the plasticity of brain operations that allows functional areas to expand can affect strength in other areas. Comparative neurological research indicates the various configurations that allow for enhanced hearing or sight or smell, for example, are related to the size of those processing areas within the brain (22–25). It seems the trade-off for Paleolithic populations, as analytic cognition expanded, was that the holistic experience was diminished. (See Hopkins, Pilcher, and Cantalupo in *Primate Psychology*, 2003, for a thorough discussion of the comparative structural similarities in the brain between human and other primates.)

Keep in mind that the transformations taking place within this time frame reflect for the most part a population still relatively balanced between analytic and holistic thought. Note Mellars' enthusiastic comment on the aesthetic creativity of the Upper Paleolithic (1994, 67):

> the art stands in many ways as the most impressive and enduring testimony to the creativity of Upper Paleolithic culture—not only in terms of the sheer skill and aesthetic flair of the artists themselves, but also in their capacity to convey highly sophisticated, symbolic messages in a remarkable variety of forms.

This enthusiasm may be tempered somewhat if these aesthetic achievements are seen as a "natural" function of a significantly holistic brain.

ANTHROPOSEMIOSIS

The analytical mind is not simply a means of organizing connections; it actively seeks organization, finding patterns even where sometimes none exist. This is sequential thinking, thinking outside the bubble. Our diagrammatic construction with lines interconnecting the bubbles themselves introduces narrative. This is the transformation that produces the mythmaking species, where bubbles can be conceived from a purely mental environment, rather than simply from the perceived world. The same mindset that foresees the outcome of the refinement of a tool form can ultimately build idea onto idea, proposition onto proposition, and construct a narrative, rather than simply recognizing event patterns.

Although for most people their thought bubbles have lost their high-definition memory recall, there are still large proportions of the human population who retain much of the full-color detail. And, it is the interactions between these two modes of cognition, these two continua, that help provide for the wonderful diversity found in all human populations in every culture.

In terms of the "human" construction of external reality, analytical dominance is illustrated by the nodes of interrelated elements of perception interconnecting across bubble boundaries. For the first time connections from event to event are analyzed in a linear fashion, as a time line from past to future. This is the sequential aspect of analytical thought (Bering and Povinelli 2003, 224) that allows for planning and true evaluation of past efforts, the search for pattern and prediction of the future (Gazzaniga 2008, 367–68), time consciousness, and the awareness of results of changes through time. Sequential thought allows for generating stories of our individual histories, our personal narrative, and the invention of narrative in general. At this point the human brain becomes involved with inventing cause-and-effect plots for personal experience and events in the external world (Bering and Povinelli 2003, 210, 228–29), and as a result, discerning annual variations in the environment and food sources leading to the first efforts at manipulation of those sources—plant and animal domestication. Finally, in our estimation this also marks the time of mythmaking, Giambattista Vico's *ingegno* fully realized (again, see note 1). It is the genesis of scientific thought, and the development of ruled-based behavior, such as the grammatical communication system that constitutes *language as a modeling system* (or, as we have called it elsewhere, Language II, Haworth and Prewitt, 2010). All of these markers manifest the underlying logical capacity of Peirce's "argument," the ultimate cognitive integration of analytical thought with abstracted traces of holistic experience.

Returning to the archaeological record, the Mesolithic era (12,000 to 8,000 BCE) appears to document a next level of transformation. The Mesolithic represents yet another progression in lithic tool technology with the appearance of microlith industries. The small blades were apparently hafted onto wood or bone elements to form a "wide-range of multi-component tools" (Mithen 1994, 96). In addition to a varied stone-tool assemblage, Mesolithic sites contain diverse tool forms of wood, bone, and antler, including points, barbed harpoons, fishhooks, woven wicker traps, and bark containers. Many of the larger pieces are adorned with geometric designs, and sculptural forms are highly stylized. These sites also provide evidence for structures and settlements, as well as the first substantial expansion of *Homo sapiens* into the New World. The first cemeteries and burials with grave goods date from the late Mesolithic (Mithen 1994, 79–135). The range of variability in the Mesolithic leads Mithen to characterize the period as being a finale to the hunter-gather era, a prelude to the economic systems of later prehistory, as well as providing an identity unique to its time and to proclaim it "one of the most critical periods of transformation in European prehistory" (1994, 133–35). In our estimation, the Mesolithic constitutes one of the most critical periods of "human" prehistory generally.

With the continued transformation in brain physiology, the holistic mode is diminished and those individuals within the population capable of the artistic achievements of the Upper Paleolithic ostensibly disappear (Mellars 1994, 78; Haworth 2007), leaving the predominant art forms for the Mesolithic and beyond to be the stylized abstractions of human cultures still prevalent today (Mithen 1994, 127–32; Haworth 2007). Unlike the startling and relatively abrupt changes noted in the archaeological record for the advent of the Upper Paleolithic, the time line for the transition to the Mesolithic and on into the Neolithic have "blurred" and "fuzzy" edges (Mithen 1994, 79). The rock art of the Spanish Levant presents a unique illustration of this continued progression (Beltrán 1982). This art, and the archaeological record in general, are indicative of a population whose brain physiology is still undergoing transformation. The end result worldwide by the advent of the Neolithic in the Old World and domestication of plants in the New World is the established analytical mind of the contemporary human species.

CAVEAT

Each time we have presented a version of this holistic to analytic scenario for human cognitive evolution, we have stressed the point that there still remains a huge diversity of cognitive types throughout humanity with talents expressed in great variety. Although analytic thought introduced new perspectives on the world, the true uniqueness of human creativity lies in the power of the combination of cognitive styles within the population and within the individual. As we have noted before, Dunn et al. (1992) researched the extent to which individuals tended toward the low or high end of the continua of both analytical and holistic modes of cognition. Regardless of the general dominance of the analytic style for most, there still remains a vibrant interaction between the two styles in each of us, allowing for the tremendous diversity of human talents. Although left/right brain explanations of human cognition have often been overplayed, especially in popular writing, Gazzaniga's studies on the comparative functions of the left and right hemispheres presents one take on the integration of analytic and holistic modes (2008, 296):

> the left-hemisphere interpreter constructs theories to assimilate perceived information into a comprehensible whole. . . . In doing so, however, the process of elaborating (story making) has a deleterious effect on the accuracy of perceptual recognition, as it does with verbal and visual material. Accuracy remains high in the right hemisphere, however, because it does not engage in these interpretive processes. The advantage of having such a dual system is obvious. The right hemisphere maintains an accurate record of events, leaving the left hemisphere free to elaborate and make inferences about the material presented. In an intact brain, the two systems complement each other, allowing elaborative processing without sacrificing veracity.

There is great variability, however, in the ways in which this combination of functions may present itself within the individual. We are not all mathematicians, or musicians, or academics. And let's not forget that our so-called success as a species may also be the cause of our ultimate demise, since contemporary technology suggests that our ability to connect between events seems limited after all. We may plan over annual cycles, but we have obviously not yet mastered concern beyond a generational limit.

One of the failures of the analytic process is a tendency to assume "like" cognitive systems in others, whether we are considering our neighbors or our neighbors' dogs. Our personal modeling system does not necessarily apply across communities or species. It is part of the pattern recognition tactic that serves us well in many pragmatic ways (Gazzaniga 2008, 368) that sends us off the mark in this manner. We take limited data and apparent similar end results and assume the internal processes that underlie them, resulting in the anthropomorphism of comparative animal studies (Rivas and Burghardt 2002), not to mention just basic human misunderstandings in our daily lives. As noted by Bering and Povenelli (2003, 209):

> the very mind (the human one) that seeks to analyze objectively the behavior of other species in order to determine the nature of their cognitive systems is already wired to interpret their behavior from a human standpoint—regardless of the objective reality. Put another way, here is one thing of which we can be sure: the human mind is extremely adept at seeing the world through its own lens.

We stress that what we see through our own personal lens affects our interpretation of *all* others, humans and other species alike. The commonalities that we share with other species through common aspects of holistic cognition and limited analytic capacities feed our tendency to overgeneralize. And thus, even possessing the derived cognitive platform that enables anthroposemiosis, vigilant awareness of cognitive variability must underlie any efforts for understanding human behavior and evolution. We therefore suggest, again, that the analytical terms of Peirce's system of sign categories help researchers avoid some of the pitfalls of anthropomorphic projection.

NOTE

1. There are parallels here with the ideas of Giambattista Vico, or at least with Marcel Danesi's (1993) interpretation of them in his book *Vico, Metaphor, and the Origin of Language*. According to Danesi, Vico's *memoria* represents the neurological system of stored ideas (51), which we consider to be represented by our bubble concept. His *ingegno*, or "invention," defined as "the faculty the conscious mind required for organizing the meaning-making units produced by the *fantasia* into new units and structures" (51), are the interconnections within the bubbles. His *fantasia*, or "imagination," as "the mind's ability to reflect on stimuli not present in the immediate environment" (50), are represented by the new bubbles that are created outside those of purely perceptual memory. And his Metaphor with a capital M, then, comprises the connections made between bubbles, creating his Surface Level cognition that overlays the Deep Level consciousness of Vico's Primitive Mind (51–55). Vico's notion of the Primitive Mind just may be embodied in the holistic thinker. However, his *memoria* is probably not our only connection here with other animals. There must be some level of *fantasia* and *ingegno* behind primate cognition, those levels of problem solving and invention necessary to the success of these species. We certainly have plenty of evidence of that, if we choose to see it. Vico's problem was seeing how these elements could exist without necessarily leading to Metaphor and the human Surface Level cognition. He saw these things as building one upon the other in a sort of miraculous transformation, a mother-may-I step, where the connections are brought into a syntactical order in and of themselves. Danesi states that *fantasia* is an "epiphenomenal product of brain activity" while *ingegno* is considered simply "a derivative of *fantasia* . . . thus not connected directly to bodily processes" (51). However, if you consider this organizational quality a physiological by-product, altered in very real ways by the increasing dominance of the analytical brain, then one does not necessarily follow the other. Once one sees the process through a shift toward analytical thinking in a development dependent upon sequencing, then one may accept indicative levels of inspiration and invention across species. Unless humans can learn to recognize and celebrate this, our self-applauded magnificent ingenuity falls flat.

WORKS CITED

Antinucci, Francesco, ed. 1989. *Cognitive Structure and Development in Nonhuman Primates*. Hillsdale, NJ: Lawrence Erlbaum Associates.

Beltrán, Antonio. 1982. *Rock Art of the Spanish Levant*. Translated by Margaret Brown. Cambridge: Cambridge University Press. (Original work published in Italian as *Da cacciatori ad allevatori l'arte rupestre del Levante Spagnolo* by Editoriale Jaca Book, Milan, 1980.)

Bering, Jesse M., and Daniel J. Povinelli. 2003. "Comparing Cognitive Development." In *Primate Psychology*, edited by Dario Maestripieri, 424–50. Cambridge, MA: Harvard University Press.

Cunliffe, Barry, ed. 1994. *The Oxford Illustrated Prehistory of Europe*. Oxford: Oxford University Press.

Danesi, Marcel. 1993. *Vico, Metaphor, and the Origin of Language*. Bloomington: Indiana University Press.

Donald, Merlin. 1991. *Origins of the Modern Mind: Three Stages in the Evolution of Culture and Cognition*. Cambridge, MA: Harvard University Press.

Dunn, Bruce R., Denise Dunn, David Andrews, and Marlin L. Languis. 1992. "Metacontrol: A Cognitive Model of Brain Functioning for Psychophysiological Study of Complex Learning." *Educational Psychologist* 27(4): 455–71.

Fossey, Dian. 1983. *Gorillas in the Mist*. Boston: Houghton Mifflin Company.

Fouts, Roger. 1997. *Next of Kin: What Chimpanzees Have Taught Me about Who We Are*. New York: William Morrow and Company.

Gazzaniga, Michael S. 2008. *Human: The Science behind What Makes Us Unique*. New York: HarperCollins Publishers.

Golding, William. 1955. *The Inheritors*. New York: Harcourt, Brace & World.

Goodall, Jane. 1986. *The Chimpanzees of Gombe: Patterns of Behavior*. Cambridge, MA: The Belknap Press of Harvard University Press.

Grandin, Temple. 1995. *Thinking in Pictures: My Life with Autism*. New York: Doubleday.

Grandin, Temple, and Catherine Johnson. 2005. *Animals in Translation: Using the Mysteries of Autism to Decode Animal Behavior*. New York: Harcourt.

Haworth, Karen A. 2006. "Upper Paleolithic Art, Autism, and Cognitive Style: Implications for the Evolution of Language." *Semiotica* 162: 1/4, 127–74.

———. 2007 "Cognitive Style and Zoosemiotics." In *Semiotics 2004/2005*, edited by Stacy Monahan, Ben Smith, and Terry Prewitt. Ottawa: Legas Press.

Haworth, Karen A., and Terry Prewitt. 2006. "Semeiotic, the Evolution of Anthroposemiosis, and the Meaning of 'Language.'" Paper presented to the Southern Anthropology Society in Pensacola Beach, Florida.

———. 2010. "Two Steps toward Semiotic Capacity, out of the Muddy Concept of Language." *Semiotica* 178: 1/4, 53–79.

Heaton, Pamela, and Gregory L. Wallace. 2004. "Annotation: The Savant Syndrome." *Journal of Child Psychology and Psychiatry* 45: 5, 899–911.

Hopkins, William D., Dawn L. Pilcher, and Claudio Cantalupo. 2003. "Brain Substrates for Communication, Cognition, and Handedness." In *Primate Psychology*, edited by Dario Maestripieri, 424–50. Cambridge, MA: Harvard University Press.

Howe, Michael J. A. 1989. *Fragments of Genius: The Strange Feats of Idiot Savants*. London: Routledge.

Köhler, Wolfgang. 1925. *The Mentality of Apes*. New York: Liveright.

———. 1947. *Gestalt Psychology: An Introduction to New Concepts in Modern Psychology*. New York: Liveright.

Jamieson, Dale. 2002. "Cognitive Ethology at the End of Neuroscience." In *The Cognitive Animal: Empirical and Theoretical Perspectives on Animal Cognition*, edited by Marc Bekoff, Colin Allen, and Gordon M. Burghardt, 69–75. Cambridge, MA: The MIT Press.

Lilly, John C. 1975. *Lilly on Dolphins: Humans of the Sea*. Garden City, NY: Anchor Books.

Mellars, Paul. 1994. "The Upper Paleolithic Revolution." In *The Oxford Illustrated Prehistory of Europe*, edited by Barry Cunliffe, 42–78. Oxford: Oxford University Press.

Mithen, Steven. 1994. "The Mesolithic Age." In *The Oxford Illustrated Prehistory of Europe*, edited by Barry Cunliffe, 79–135. Oxford: Oxford University Press.

Morton, Eugene S., and Jake Page. 1992. *Animal Talk: Science and the Voices of Nature*. New York: Random House.

NEWSER. "Animal Intelligence." http://www.newser.com/tag/31304/1/animal-inellignce.html?utm_source=ssp&utm_medium=cpc&utm_campaign=tag.

Peirce, Charles Sanders. 1867 [1984]. "On the Natural Classification of Arguments." In *Writings of Charles S. Peirce: A Chronological Edition*, edited by Edward Moore, Volume 2, 1867–1871, 23–48. Bloomington: Indiana University Press.

———. 1867a [1984]. "On a New List of Categories." In *Writings of Charles S. Peirce: A Chronological Edition*, edited by Edward Moore, Volume 2, 1867–1871, 49–59. Bloomington: Indiana University Press.

Prince-Hughes, Dawn. 2001. *Gorillas among Us: A Primate Ethnographer's Book of Days*. Tucson: University of Arizona Press.

———. 2004. *Songs of the Gorilla Nation: My Journey through Autism*. New York: Harmony Books.

Rivas, Jesús, and Gordon M. Burghardt. 2002. "Crotalomorphism: A Metaphor for Understanding Anthropomorphism by Omission." In *The Cognitive Animal: Empirical and Theoretical Perspectives on Animal Cognition*, edited by Marc Bekoff, Colin Allen, and Gordon M. Burghardt, 9–17. Cambridge, MA: MIT Press.

Russon, Anne E., and David R. Begun. 2004. "Evolutionary Origins of Great Ape Intelligence: An Integrated Overview." In *The Evolution of Thought: Evolutionary Origins of Great Ape Intelligence*, edited by Anne E. Russon and David R. Begun, 353–55. Cambridge: Cambridge University Press.

Savage-Rumbaugh, Sue, Stuart G. Shanker, and Talbot J. Taylor. 1998. *Apes, Language, and the Human Mind*. New York: Oxford University Press.

Sebeok, Thomas A. 1972. *Perspectives in Zoosemiotics*. The Hague: Mouton.

———. 1974. "Semiotics: A Survey of the State of the Art." In *Linguistics and Adjacent Arts and Sciences*, Vol. 12 of the *Current Trends in Linguistics* series, 211–64. The Hague: Mouton.

Sebeok, Thomas A., and Robert Rosenthal, eds. 1981. *Clever Hans Phenomenon: Communication with Horses, Whales, Apes, and People*. New York: New York Academy of Sciences.

Sebeok, Thomas A., and Jean Umiker-Semeok, eds. 1980. *Speaking of Apes: A Critical Anthology of Two-Way Communication with Man*. New York: Plenum.

Selfe, Lorna. 1977. *Nadia: A Case of Extraordinary Drawing Ability in an Autistic Child*. London: Academic Press.

Treffert, Darold A., and Gregory L. Wallace. 2002. "Islands of Genius." *Scientific American* (June 2002): 76–85.

Walker, Matt. 2009. "Chimps Mentally Map Fruit Trees." BBC Earth News, June 8. http://news.bbc.co.uk/earh/hi/earth_news/newsid_8086000/8086246.stm.

Chapter Eleven

Semiotics of Human Evolution

Terry's Story: In the preceding chapters, we have presented a background for asserting the importance of cognitive style with respect to the development of the unique aspects of the human species. The work has indeed evolved over years of revision to arrive at this concise treatment. Through our personal processes, as Karen and I also established our own basis for accurately sharing ideas, we arrived at a semiotic terminology that we felt best reflected the cognitive transformations within the hominid line, while opening up means of examining the cultural phenomena of our archaeological legacy. Our discussions were sometimes intense, and I recall now how strange and frustrating they may have been for our students, colleagues, and others to witness. I recall with laughter one particularly intense discussion of synaptic elaborations of the brain while on the way to the university with our five-year-old grandson in a car seat behind us; at a pause in the conversation, we heard the young voice behind us saying, "Yeah yeah, yeah yeah, yeah yeah." There were, no doubt, adults who had a similar reaction. But I now feel more comfortable drafting a more accessible culminating argument for our particular view of human evolution seen through the lens of the analytic/holistic dichotomy and the transformation of the human brain through time.

This all-important transformation relies on the unique development among hominids that is one of Homo sapiens defining characteristics, the exceptional enlargement of the brain, far beyond the trend of cerebral enlargement of the primates in general. To open the narrative, we need to provide our views of what initiated the dynamic changes of the hominid brain. The synopsis of the evolutionary sequence offered here is based upon our various articles and lectures, especially our 2010 article on the evolution of semiotic capacity in the journal Semiotica, *parts of which formed the working structure for this chapter. Since that writing we have developed some of the ideas, and also come to some different conclusions. And this renegotiation of the material may be kinder to more general readers, while attempting to remain true to essential technical details. Hopefully, we have succeeded in establishing the appropriate background. Moving on toward a general conclusion, with this chapter we present a personal synthesis, recognizing that our results are more suggestive than definitive.*

BIPEDALISM AND THE BRAIN

Bipedal locomotion, one of the primary physical abilities of the hominid family, began around 5 million years ago and was established in efficient forms by about 2.5 million years ago.[1] The earliest bipeds in Africa, members of the genus *Australopithecus*, clearly manifested one of the common differentiating adjustments of other anthropoid ape populations, becoming separated into small- and large-bodied variants. The large-bodied forms died out in the mid- to late-Pleistocene, while the small-bodied forms represent the group of lineages from which the genus *Homo* emerged. While the cranial size of these australopithecines was comparable to the modern apes—about 500 cubic centimeter brains in adults—the post-cranial skeleton is comparable to humans in possessing a fully developed upright posture complex. The fossil australopithecines establish clearly that upright posture and pelvic modifications preceded any dramatic enlargement of the hominid brain.

Hominid upright posture restructured the pelvis into a box-shaped form with a much narrower birth canal than is found in modern or fossil apes. One of the strong osteological traits used in identifying sex among efficient bipeds is the greater sciatic notch of the ilium. The wider notch among females keeps the birth canal somewhat more open than in males, counteracting in part the much more prominent trend toward pelvic closure. Early on, however, any pelvic constriction meant that birth for the small-bodied australopithecines would have been slightly more difficult than among other apes, including the large-bodied bipeds.

One of the early fossils establishing australopithecines as hominids was the famous "Taung child," an *Australopithicus africanus* of perhaps three years of age. Compared to a chimpanzee of presumed similar age, we see in both a slight juvenile projection of the lower face (prognathism) and a less prominent cranial vault than in a human infant. The Taung fossil nonetheless looks more human than older australopithecines, or than any juvenile modern ape. We know that a chimpanzee newborn will develop substantial motor skills almost immediately after birth, and we may presume that australopithecine infants also developed rather quickly. However, though the brain of a human fetus is slightly larger than either an australopithecine or a chimpanzee at birth, it still has yet to achieve a large part of its overall surface area growth and synaptic development, and its motor skills are not well developed in the first weeks of life. Compared to apes, human are born very "premature." We suggest that closure of the birth canal in small-bodied australopithecines created a moderate incompatibility with cranial size at birth within the typical brain ontogeny for the species. In simpler terms, these hominid ancestors would have started bearing slightly more premature infants.

Two adaptive solutions for the problem of premature infants in hominids appear to have helped shape our evolution. First, a general increase in body size produced an absolutely larger birth canal, as occurred with the large-bodied *Australopithecus robustus*. The robust forms, pursuing an apparently vegetarian diet, offer something of a parallel to the modern gorilla, though these forms disappear by the mid-Pleistocene. There is little early evidence on australopithecine ecology, but dental evidence suggests that *Australopithecus africanus* had a richer protein diet, and the lineage of *Homo* beyond that shows progressive involvement in hunting and meat eating. In later African populations, a body size increase occurred for the genus *Homo* soon after its emergence.[2] We may presume that body mass increases would have encountered limits based on body-temperature regulation.[3]

The second adaptive solution is more complex. Primate evolutionary grades have all tended toward more complex nervous systems than their ancestor populations. For the small-bodied australopithecines, a larger mass of cerebral cortex in adults would accommodate the cooperation and learning processes supportive of caring for premature infants. Care of infants would have been particularly important, since the hominoid forms already had the number of offspring typically reduced to single infant gestations of long duration. Postnatal care by adults also would have slowed population replacement, making infant care a major factor in demographic continuity. Such a situation is suggested, of course, by the very slow population growth of the entire Paleolithic. We suggest that the "kick" to the expansion of the hominid cerebral cortex came with species like *Australopithecus africanus*. It is not difficult to see that such conditions would have provided impetus for increased problem-solving ability, and hence a more complex nervous system.

The actual difference in the human and chimpanzee genome is very small, though the cognitive qualities in the two species emerge from differences in the quantity of neurons, for the hominid lineage about twice the number than in the hominoids (Sapolsky 2006). The differences among these related species also involve timing of the development processes, with genetic factors controlling the timing of an otherwise generalized neuronal growth. Larger brains in the context of upright posture, from this point of view, do not suggest the emergence of complex new kinds of neurons or specialized tissues. This certainly supports the idea of similar hominoid-hominid development toward symbolic communication capacities, grounded by behavioral evidence that is highly consistent with zoosemiotic approaches to animal capacities (see Fouts and Waters 2001; Fouts and Jensvold 2002).

Human and chimpanzee absolute fetal growth is roughly comparable at term, although the chimp already has a cranial capacity approaching hominoid limits. The human, however, still has substantial brain growth and motor development to achieve after birth, while the chimpanzee is born with much greater motor ability, reflecting major differences in the early timing of ontogeny. The slowed maturation process in the human accommodates later neural development through the processes of synaptogenesis and myelination, which radically expands the brain after birth, but at a cost of early infant independence. This slowed ontogeny, the "tolerative adaptation" allowing greater neurological complexity, is often referred to as neoteny (Clark 1971 provides discussion of tolerative adaptations for several functional complexes in primate evolution).

Viewing the general size and size-range development of the hominid brain, we see that there has been approximately a thousand cubic centimeter overall increase in adult brain volume since the time of the australopithecines. The first documented jump in size away from the hominoid pattern came with *Homo habilis* some 1.8 million years ago, and it is appropriate for us to ask why this increase occurred. We suggest that the pelvic narrowing associated with upright posture had the effect of creating several simultaneous adjustments in the nervous systems of the populations leading to the genus *Homo*. First, there would have been at least moderate fetal-maternal incompatibility for all of the early bipeds, resulting in more premature births in the small-bodied forms. Premature infants would have had less-developed motor abilities, and thus would have presented a survival problem for the adults in the population. We know that modern gorillas and chimps remain dependent upon the mother for at least two years, but these young have well-developed motor abilities. If premature infants among hominids were motor-deficient for a longer period of time, they would require even greater attention and care from the adults than modern apes show. The biological response to such a problem, following the primate trend, would be to elaborate the cerebral cortex.

The adaptive response leading to a larger brain would certainly have exacerbated the problem of pelvic disproportion for the genus *Homo*. In a complex secondary adaptation, the need to balance between cranial size at birth and the pelvis supporting upright posture, we believe, pushed the human lineage into a series of adjustments for the maturation cycle. The trend toward greater cortical mass involved not only a greater number of neurons, but also enhanced synaptic connections responding to the stimulus-rich environment from birth through juvenile stages of development. We know that modern humans undergo substantial postnatal neuronal specialization. The actual changes in earlier populations were much more complex than this, taking the form of a sculpting process through which bundles of neurons acquired different functions (see Nelson and Collins 2001, 3-44). The problems involved in brain specialization also involve "multifocal" neuronal connections more than "function-specific" neuronal bundles (see Lieberman 2002, 38-40 and 46-47).[4] Even so, for our purposes here, we merely stress that the hominid brain creates more neurons than other higher primates during early fetal development, in a relatively unspecialized mass reproduction of neuronal tissues (again, see Sapolsky 2006).

Turning to consideration of specialized areas, Roger Fouts notes tissue asymmetries in chimpanzee brains (*Pan troglodytes*) suggesting structures similar to Broca's and Wernicke's areas and the angular gyrus. If such structures are incipient in the hominoid evolutionary grade, and potentially supportive of related species-specific capacities of cognitive processing (Fouts and Waters 2001), this would underscore the potential for complex sign functions in other higher primates. Additionally, subcortical (mid-brain and brain stem) tissues may also be important to communication functions in humans (see Lieberman 2002, 40), and presumably also to our closest ape relatives. These adjustments of the brain and locomotor complexes for early humans seem to have occurred amid continuing trends of neoteny involving adaptations that expanded the life span, increased body size, slowed ontogeny, readjusted the points of birth and sexual maturity in the populations, and greatly expanded the period of postnatal neuronal development, and hence, the intensive care by adults during infant/child phases of development. Neoteny was emphasized by Clark (1971) in his discussions of the emergent human lineage, and more recent discussions of this important evolutionary process have elaborated on its importance (see Somel, Franz, Yan et al. 2009; Somel, Tang, and Khitovich 2011).

In summary, the constraints of the derived upright posture commitment pushed brain increases among early hominids, leading to an animal with enhanced semiosic, as well as incipient semiotic capacities. Such a cycle of events, we believe, is signaled by technological developments, with the "modeling" capacities of the later genus *Homo* becoming foundational to fully human anthroposemiosis, and ultimately, supporting changes that refocused the human mind onto its secondary linguistic medium. With such a reflexive evolutionary development, the cognized reality of the animal (the *Umwelt*) would become dominated by the behavioral and signal system it enabled (language), creating shared variants of species-specific experience (*Lebenswelt*). In short, we *became "cultural" beings as a secondary consequence of neoteny, through which symbolling capacities fed back onto basic problem-solving capacities to produce full-blown semiotic systems.*

Our zoosemiotic arguments about infant care and ontogeny should also account for demonstrated semiosic capacities in the great apes, abilities that remain somewhat behaviorally incipient in the wild, but that appear to parallel human symbol manipulation (language as communication) in captive populations. The extended infant care necessary for the great apes is well attested for wild and captive populations through natural abilities for imitative learning, problem solving, and direct communication (see, for example, Goodall 1986; Fouts 1997; Savage-Rumbaugh 1986; Savage-Rumbaugh et al. 1998). The biological foundation of emergent human abilities must take into account such close species parallels, behavioral and genetic, at least with the African apes, if not also to the wider grade of the Hominoidea generally.

STAGES OF HOMINID COGNITIVE EVOLUTION

The broad view of hominid brain evolution suggests at least a two-stage process. With the appearance of *Homo habilis* came the first clear evidence of increases of the cerebral cortex, although there was a relatively quick establishment of the somewhat larger and elongated brain of *Homo erectus* and contemporary populations of the later Lower Paleolithic. The transformation from the *Homo erectus* evolutionary grade to *Homo sapiens* presents several complexities. We suggest that there were at least two, and possibly three components to this later process. First, European Neanderthals and other Middle Paleolithic populations have been variously interpreted (see Aiello and Dunbar 1993; Stringer and Gamble 1993; Cunliffe 1994; Johanson and Edgar 1996; Tattersall and Schwartz 2001).[5] Current discussions are much more open to the idea that there were several competing subspecies or regional populations during the Middle Paleolithic, presenting potentially different capacities of semiosis locally, but based upon a generally common genetic heritage (i.e., cladistic associations). Very likely, most of these populations, especially those outside Africa, were part of a broad punctuated equilibrium process leading to our species. This is strongly supported by the global distribution of these hominids, as well as *Homo sapiens* by forty thousand years ago. Within this field of parallel populations, we accept the classic European Neanderthals as one of the most specialized derived forms, based upon their distinctive cranial features and large average cranial capacity. Such distinctiveness, however, is merely a part of the less well-known complex physiological variability of the relatively short Middle Paleolithic era. The key observation for this group should be the potential for some, if not most, of these groups contributing to the emergence of *Homo sapiens* if not through direct sharing of local and regional adaptations through gene flow, then through cladistic parallelisms. Thus, from the perspective of the transition from prominent holistic to dominant analytic thought, we identify the Archaic members of the genus *Homo* (including Neanderthals) as a transitional form between the evolutionary grades of *Homo erectus* and *Homo sapiens sapiens*. This relatively simplified classification also agrees with the general sense of technological developments from the Lower Paleolithic (Acheulean and Chopper traditions) to the diverse Middle Paleolithic technologies, and onward to the tools we call Upper Paleolithic.

From a semiotic perspective, the Lower Paleolithic for us remains consistent with typical animal semiosis, based mainly in iconic and indexical signs at a pre-symbolic level. With the Middle Paleolithic, however, the complexity of tool-production processes implies some potential for the emergence of symbols, though there are practically no other physical evidences of symbol use (we take this problem up later in this discussion). Finally, with the Upper Paleolithic we encounter clear use of symbolic rhemes among the iconic depictions of cave art. However, as we have observed, Upper Paleolithic cave art lacks suggestions of narrative or depictions of human actors, weapons, hunting, emotional states, or motion. On this basis, we propose a stage in the development of human cognition, after the establishment of skeletally modern *Homo sapiens sapiens*, when humans were capable of higher cognitive functions but did not universally and habitually employ signs at the level of symbols or linguistically grounded semiotic arguments. In this view, technology becomes as important as physiology in assessing how today's *Homo sapiens* gained our unique engagement with symbols.

Considering that in Europe and Africa, the late "archaic" Homo sapiens and Neanderthal populations still possessed similarities to Acheulean assemblages, anthropologists have always recognized technological developments as a cumulative process. If specific tools forms represent *technological equivalents* of iconic rhemes or dicents (see again Chapter 9, and Prewitt and Haworth 2004), it would seem for modern humans only a small step to suggest vocal or manual use of symbolic rhemes to reinforce the forms of materials and their functions. Such a step, however, is not necessary for the technology to be effective. The celebrated forms of Lavallois technology illustrate a strongly iconic aesthetic by a species that is functioning primarily in the holistic cognitive mode. Core reduction processes, such as those described by Kuhn (1995) do not rely upon symbolic reinforcements, as long as the step-by-step process proceeds from immediate observations and memory functions. We can suggest that Mousterian tools link visual/material forms to behavioral functions in at least potentially "conventional" ways, since flake selection and shaping are certainly not random. For the tool user and later the archaeologist, the form becomes an index of function, as opposed to seeking an edge attribute on a multipurpose tool.

The technological processes of the Mousterian, then, dating from perhaps 120,000 to 40,000 years ago, are not only notable in that they represent a transition between the Lower and Upper Paleolithic, but also because they represent a potential juncture in the emergence of symbolic capacities. A question we should also ask is: Does a reduction process aimed at producing particular "shapes" and "kinds" of flakes parallel the hierarchic and analytical process involved in syntax? What impresses those who work with Mousterian tools is the essential "beauty" of the artifacts, an aesthetic expressive of the same kinds of clean precision seen in the cave paintings of later archaeological manifestations. We may also ask how much "propositional" value do stone reduction processes offer toward some sense of complex syntax? Is the process a series of steps conceived as unfolding events with many potentials, or a holistic process conceived as linking point A to point B only by some required series of outcomes. In our view, a staged reduction process, paired with construction of composite tools, which we know characterizes stone technology from the later Upper Paleolithic onward, precisely parallels structure as we encounter it in language. Such a process calls for greater intentionality and "linear" cognitive focus, while also taking advantage of accidental production of desired results (for a cognitively grounded exposition of this generalization, see especially Young and Bonnichsen 1984).[6]

Thus, though Middle Paleolithic knappers were beginning to create a "tool kit," the technology did not necessitate a major shift in cognitive capacities. The indexical "propositions" entailed in the attributes of the Acheulean axe were merely divested onto separable units, and so the tool's "propositional" value in an instance of usage was specific, and apparently somewhat fixed. The technology increased the efficiency of material use and conservation, and perhaps made visual selection of appropriate edges for particular tasks easier. A "user" of a particular "tool" (as we say, the "right" tool) is acting out the proposition created by the tool's attributes in relation to what it can accomplish. But a tool is not necessarily a "proposition" until it is picked up with intention, just as a word doesn't "mean" any particular thing until it is placed in syntax. Still, tools can exist as indices of the propositions that created them. In archaeological contexts, tools may also be read as propositions about action sequences or intention in patterned motor behavior (Young and Bonnichsen 1984, 21–87). Overall, however, production of a differentiated tool kit has strong implications for the analytical cognitive abilities of the animal, but it is not definitive proof that the elements of technology were being reified in symbolic forms.

As the complexity of tools increases, including manufacture of compound tools from diverse materials, the elaborations suggest that more than simple imitative modes in learning or direct rhematic-symbolic reference are involved (see also Mithen 1996, 208–16). As we have seen (Chapter 9), the Upper Paleolithic outside Europe involved diverse processes of development involving different trajectories of novel and established practices (again see Brantingham, Kuhn, and Kerry 2004). With the late Upper Paleolithic tradition, stone tools appear to become "styled" within regions and components, offering signs of "convention" and the opening to all the symbolic complexity of our world. Cave paintings and portable art of that period, continuing through the late Upper Paleolithic, suggests that holistic experience still dominated production of the materials in the archaeological record. Even so, the stylistic explosion of the late Upper Paleolithic, commonly linked mainly to the Aurignacian and Magdalenian periods in Europe, is a change with major cognitive implications. Specifically, diverse arbitrary local elaborations in stone tools beyond functionality indicate another important change involving a growing dominance of analytical-sequential cognitive processing. And biologically, later Upper Paleolithic populations in Europe and Eurasia are undoubtedly at least in cladistic biological association throughout the Old World, presenting a consistently rich complex behavior set accompanied by clear physiological differences from Middle Paleolithic populations. This situation reinforces the idea that early use of rhematic symbols and dicents influenced behavior sufficiently to give impetus to analytical dominance.

As we have argued elsewhere (Chapter 9; Prewitt and Haworth 2004; Haworth 2006; Haworth and Prewitt 2006, 2010), the wide sweep of elaborations of tools, art, and other material patterns of *Homo sapiens* during the Upper Paleolithic, sometimes appearing essentially alongside Neanderthal manifestations, shows a very different quality of mind from both earlier species and adjacent Middle Paleolithic populations. This is certainly observed in the Chatelperronian complex of Spain. But the populations who followed in the later stages of the Upper Paleolithic (after about 25,000 BCE), and on into the Mesolithic and Neolithic, were all dramatically more complex. It is in these later manifestations that definitive evidence of habitual symbolling appears. Working with the earlier populations, Mithen (2006, 233) has come to very similar conclusions as ours based upon cultural and neurophysiological evidence.

SOME GENERAL COMMENTS ON SEMIOTIC UNFOLDING

We have discussed earlier in this book the extraordinary similarity of Upper Paleolithic cave art to the artistic productions of autistic savants and the cognitive implications of this similarity for the evolution of language (see also Haworth 2006, 2007; Haworth and Prewitt 2006). Out of this work, we contend, regardless of the specific variations in the connections that may genetically occur in the human brain, that *one* aspect of autism is a more holistic mode of brain functioning. We have drawn on the work of contemporary holistic thinkers to support the idea that such functioning has something in common not only with other animal species, but with our immediate ancestors. We are certainly not suggesting that Paleolithic people were "autistic"—instead, we are arguing that there are signs of holistic brain function that suggest an absence at least of habitual or dedicated verbal language in the experience of our immediate evolutionary ancestors. But a brain allowing emphasis of analytical functions over holistic processing is precisely the kind of organ that could ultimately give rise to the human *Lebenswelt*, as Deely (1982, 1990, 1994, 2001) defines it, in the context of a communication system derived from the semiotic modeling capacity. Indeed, given the other indications of complex structure in technology and motor behavior, as well as physiological changes in the *Homo sapiens* brain supporting Aurignacian and Magdalenian cultures, we believe the authors of the cave art were cognitively capable of verbal symbolling, and even used it to an extent. What was lacking in practice, for a time at least, was the *habitual* use of speech to create and share symbolic arguments.

We have not taken up in this volume the origin of what linguists call "duality of patterning," the appearance of a finite structured sound system supporting an unlimited potential of rhematic symbols operating within syntax. On one level the question is irrelevant, since the vehicle employed for symbolling is less critical than the capacity of creating conventional shared meanings between individuals, as the ape language experiments have thoroughly demonstrated. But discriminating sounds and parsing the sound stream is not totally irrelevant, inasmuch as vocal communication is extant and has clearly been the main vehicle of human symbolling coming out of our evolution. One argument about how phonemic structures emerged is that sound structure is "exapted" from visual capacities for discrimination and resolution. Exaptation is merely the repurposing of an existing derived neural capacity for a different sensory or behavioral function (see, for example, Gould 1991). Since primates in general have highly developed visual systems, especially as the system accommodates dynamic discriminations, it is not a stretch to argue for those neural networks supporting elaboration of sound stream discriminations, moving from foundational calls to full-blown speech (see, for example, Ghazanfar and Takahashi 2014). The important broad review of relevant comparative biological studies has periodically been taken up by W. Tecumseh Fitch (2000, 2018). In any event, our synthesis of capacities leaves this interesting and rich area for dedicated research. We focus, instead, on hypotheses about stages in language development based upon material associations in the archaeological record.

In philosophical terms, we can call the emergent level of symbolic capacities (or human *Innenwelt* without *Lebenswelt*) "language" to the extent any information is shared as conventional association of a symbol to its referent. This is consistent with ordinary usage of the term "language," even if the symbol operates essentially as a *context-specific index*, a sign calling attention to some aspect of an ongoing situation. We envision a time when most symbols used by our ancestors worked in this way. For us, the Aurignacian presents something more like a "dawn" of semiotic consciousness, but without those special abilities being expanded into full-blown expressions of symbolic modeling. However, just as the Middle Paleolithic represented a short phase of mainly physiological transition—a step in a biological punctuated equilibrium process—the Aurignacian and similar manifestations evidently represented an even more rapid punctuated change of cognitive style accommodating the new brain physiology. We must emphasize that holistic and analytic consciousness were, during this transition, in relative balance. There can be little doubt from the evidence, however, that what we encounter in the latest Upper Paleolithic and Mesolithic is fully "human" in the sense we experience humanity, that spoken language was becoming a common feature of life, and that "shared culture" began to structure the lives of diverse communities. Beyond the later Upper Paleolithic and the Mesolithic, the *Lebenswelt as semiotic* has fully arrived, and the human animal is realizing its species-specific, inventive potential.

We offer, then, a proposed summary sequence for the evolution of language based upon semiotic constructs, our proposed transformation from holistic to analytic consciousness, observed changes in brain physiology, and the material record:

I. (5 to 2 million years ago) Separation of a small-bodied upright biped whose pelvic size provided the "kick" for a major nervous system expansion for its descendants in the genus *Homo*.

II. (2 to 1 million years ago) Accommodation of bipedal, larger-brained adaptations through increased body size, supported by a combination of cooler Pleistocene weather and an increasingly protein-rich omnivorous diet.

III. (1 million to 175,000 years ago) Dispersal of the successful and genetically variable lower Pleistocene hominid populations accompanied by differentiations of many small populations, with gene flow supporting some locally unique nervous system adaptations enhancing natural hominid tendencies to tool use, but producing mainly very general reduction technologies dependent upon iconic and indexical pattern emphasis (i.e., the Acheulean and Chopper "traditions").

IV. (175,000 to 35,000 years ago) A transformation in diverse populations across Africa, Europe, and Asia toward more linear and hierarchic tool-production processes, probably accompanied by vocal indexing, and likely manual or vocal symbolic rhemes deployed in limited combinations as "propositional" behavior. This stage suggests brain expansion supporting dicent modeling functions within a prominent holistic mode of consciousness. It is during this period that the underpinnings of the speech system most likely emerged, as vocal indexing came into common use.

V. (40,000 to 20,000 years ago) Enhancement of neural connections leading to greater verbal expression of propositional behavior through symbolic rhemes and dicents, and greater sharing of semiosic capacities of the elaborated "analytic consciousness." The archaeological record suggests that people relied increasingly upon vocal behaviors but still retained an essentially holistic mode of experiencing the Umwelt through a generalized, only moderately shared *Lebenswelt*.

VI. (20,000 to present) The habituation and elaboration of verbal expressions of semiotic consciousness, the full-blown emergence of spoken language via the capacity for the symbolic argument, narrative, emergence of diverse linguistic systems, development of elaborate traditions, aesthetic abstraction and elaboration, and other cultural elements consistent with anthroposemiosis as we know it. At this stage, the communication system serves more iconic (i.e., metaphorical) interests rather than purely indexical cueing, and we see the beginnings of cultural differentiation that may be identified with a *Lebenswelt* clearly under the dominant influence of language as a modeling system.

VII. We offer yet a final stage, which may go back almost as far as the symbolic argument, wherein the co-evolution of physical symbols, sometimes derived from icons, are a major manifestation of cultural developments. We tend to think of formal "writing" as coming much later in time, but there is growing evidence that *systems* of symbolic marks in various forms go back to perhaps 10,000 BCE, and that some symbols associated with known writing systems are likely much older (see Rudgley 1999, 72–85). The recent dating of a symbolic mark associated with the Mousterian time frame (i.e., in our stage IV) is certainly suggestive (again see Hoffmann, Standish et al. 2018).

NOTES

1. Myriad classifications and discussions of hominid development are available. For this treatment we have used as general background, because of their accessibility to non-specialists, the recent work by Ian Tattersall and Jeffrey Schwartz, *Extinct Humans* (2001), and the excellent synthesis of some key fossils by Donald Johanson and Blake Edgar, *From Lucy to Language* (1996). We also provide occasional more specific technical citations relating to particular points made along the way.

2. One of the type specimens of *Homo ergaster*, dated at 1.6 million years ago, suggests an adult height well over five feet. Beyond *Homo habilis*, most of the fossil hominids are comparatively larger, an adaptation that may have occurred also to accommodate climatic changes (see Johanson and Edgar 1996), especially global cooling of the Pleistocene.

3. Bergmann's rule covers size limitations of organisms in cold or warm climates, and Allen's rule covers optimal shapes for thermal regulation. Together, they account for a wide range of physical variations in humans and other species.

4. Philip Lieberman's synthesis of issues involved with neurophysiology and function relative to human language is a necessary ground for any zoosemiotic discussion of potentials for various kinds of sign use among the hominoids.

5. We also encourage our colleagues and students to read, or re-read William Golding's provocative novella, *The Inheritors* (1955), an early literary reflection upon the relationship between Neanderthals and Homo sapiens, which in spite of some of its dated descriptors, nicely explores the notion of a species on the brink of "language."

6. See also the provocative short essay by Ben James (2018) suggesting that linguistic structures might be derived from neuronal exaptation from established flint-knapping processes.

WORKS CITED

Aiello, Leslie C., and Robin I. M. Dunbar. 1993. "Neocortex Size, Group Size, and the Evolution of Language." *Current Anthropology* 34: 2.

Brantingham, P. Jeffrey, Steven L. Kuhn, and Kristopher W. Kerry, eds. 2004. *The Early Upper Paleolithic beyond Western Europe*. Berkeley: University of California Press.

Clark, W. E. Le Gros. 1971. *Antecedents of Man*, 3rd edition. Chicago: Quadrangle Books.

Cunliffe, Barry W. 1994. *The Oxford Illustrated Prehistory of Europe*. Oxford: Oxford University Press.

Deely, John N. 1982. *Introducing Semiotic: Its History and Doctrine*. Bloomington: Indiana University Press.

———. 1990. *Basics of Semiotics*. Bloomington: Indiana University Press.

———. 1994. *The Human Use of Signs or Elements of Anthroposemiosis*. Lanham, MD: Rowman & Littlefield.
———. 2001. *Four Ages of Understanding*. Toronto: University of Toronto Press.
Fitch, W. Tecumseh. 2000. "The Evolution of Speech: A Comparative Review." *Trends in Cognitive Science* 4: 258–67.
———. 2018. "The Biology and Evolution of Speech: A Comparative Analysis." *Annual Review of Linguistics* 4: 255–79.
Fouts, Roger S. 1997. *Next of Kin: What Chimpanzees Have Taught Me about Who We Are*. New York: William Morrow.
Fouts, Roger S., and Mary Lee Jensvold. 2002. "Armchair Delusions v. Empirical Realities: A Neurological Model for the Continuity of Ape and Human Languaging." In *Probing Human Origins*, edited by M. Goodman and A. A. Moffat, 87–101. Cambridge, MA: The American Association for the Arts and Science Press.
Fouts, Roger S., and Gabriel S. Waters. 2001. "Chimpanzee Sign Language and Darwinian Continuity: Evidence for a Neurology Continuity of Language." *Neurological Research* 23: 787–94.
Ghazanfar, Asif A., and Daniel Y. Takahashi. 2014. "The Evolution of Speech: Vision, Rhythm, Cooperation." *Trends in Cognitive Sciences* 18(10): October.
Golding, William. 1955. *The Inheritors*. New York: Harcourt, Brace, and World.
Goodall, Jane. 1986. *The Chimpanzees of Gombe: Patterns of Behavior*. Cambridge, MA: Belknap Press of Harvard University Press.
Gould, S. J. 1991. "Exaptation: A Crucial Tool for Evolutionary Psychology." *Journal of Social Issues* 47: 43–65.
Haworth, Karen A. 2006. "Upper Paleolithic Art, Autism, and Cognitive Style: Implications for the Evolution of Language." *Semiotica* 162: 1/4, 127–74.
———. 2007. "Cognitive Style and Zoosemiotics." In *Semiotics 2004/2005*, edited by Stacy Monahan, Ben Smith, and Terry Prewitt. Ottawa: Legas Press.
Haworth, Karen A., and Terry Prewitt. 2006. "Semeiotic, the Evolution of Anthroposemiosis, and the Meaning of 'Language.'" Paper presented to the Southern Anthropology Society in Pensacola Beach, Florida.
———. 2010. "Two Steps toward Semiotic Capacity, out of the Muddy Concept of Language." *Semiotica* 178: 1/4, 53–79.
Hoffmann, D. L., C. D. Standish, et al. 2018. "U-Th Dating of Carbonate Crusts Reveals Neandertal Origin of Iberian Cave Art." *Science* 359, no. 6378: 912–15.
James, Ben. 2018. "A Sneaky Theory of Where Language Came From." *The Atlantic*, June 10.
Johanson, Donald, and Blake Edgar. 1996. *From Lucy to Language*. New York: Simon & Schuster.
Kuhn, Steven. 1995. *Mousterian Lithic Technology*. Princeton, NJ: Princeton University Press.
Lieberman, Philip. 2002. "On the Nature and Evolution of the Neural Bases of Human Language." In *Yearbook of Physical Anthropology*. American Association of Physical Anthropologists (available online at www.interscience.wiley.com).
Mithen, Steven. 1996. "Social Learning and Cultural Tradition: Interpreting Early Paleolithic Technology." In *The Archaeology of Human Ancestry: Power, Sex*

and Tradition, edited by James Steele and Stephen Shennon, 207–29. New York: Routledge.
———. 2006. *The Singing Neanderthals: The Origins of Music, Language, Mind, and Body*. Cambridge, MA: Harvard University Press.
Nelson, Charles A., and Monica L. Collins. 2001. *Handbook of Developmental Cognitive Neuroscience*. Cambridge, MA: MIT Press.
Prewitt, Terry, and Karen Haworth. 2004. "The Minimal Conditions of 'Argument': Semiotics of Paleolithic Technology, Animal Tool Use, and Ape Signing in Relation to Human Language Origins." Paper presented at the annual meeting of the Southern Anthropological Society in Decatur, Georgia.
Rudgley, Richard. 1999. *The Lost Civilizations of the Stone Age*. New York: Simon & Schuster.
Sapolsky, Robert. 2006. "The 2% Difference." *Discover* (April): 42–45.
Savage-Rumbaugh, Sue. 1986. *Ape Language: From Conditioned Response to Symbol*. New York: Columbia University Press.
Savage-Rumbaugh, Sue, Stuart G. Shanker, and Talbot J. Taylor. 1998. *Apes, Language, and the Human Mind*. Oxford: Oxford University Press.
Somel, Mehmet, Henriette Franz, Zheng Yan, et al. 2009. "Transcriptional Neoteny in the Human Brain." In *Proceedings of the National Academy of Sciences* 106.14: 5743–48.
Somel, Mehmet, Lin Tang, and Philipp Khitovich. 2011. "The Role of Neoteny in Human Evolution: From Genes to the Phenotype." In *Post-genome Biology of Primates*, edited by Hirohisa Hirai, Hiroo Imai, and Yasuhiro Go, 23–41. Tokyo: Springer.
Stringer, C. B., and C. Gamble. 1993. *In Search of the Neanderthals: Solving the Puzzle of Human Origins*. London: Thames & Hudson.
Tattersall, Ian, and Jeffrey Schwartz. 2001. *Extinct Humans*. New York: Westview.
Young, David E., and Robson Bonnichsen. 1984. *Understanding Stone Tools: A Cognitive Approach*. Orono: University of Maine.

Chapter Twelve

Finding Time

Karen's Story: By the time Terry and I had established for ourselves a semiotic reading of the archaeological record, we offered several conference papers and journal articles on these ideas, because our take on human evolution now colored our thinking on almost everything. I had at that point a rather naïve notion that our arguments would eventually catch on with others and further research would ensue. While we generally received polite and mildly interested responses from other academics, no one saw our points as relating sufficiently to their own studies to warrant a change in their path. Terry was not at all surprised by this reception in academia, as he recognized how suggested changes in direction seldom obtain traction with others.

I kept seeing a need for new direction in many areas of scholarship, in research and pedagogy, and even in human interaction in general. I was beginning to realize that if I wanted our notions to have a wider audience, we would just have to make the effort ourselves to reach beyond conferences and journals. We discussed organization for a book and produced any number of outlines, none of which seemed to be adequate for presenting this rather complex argument in an accessible fashion. In the end, the deciding factor for our writing, offering an argument augmented by narratives of personal and sometime serendipitous experience, came out of yet another quirky happenstance.

I had begun to wonder about how the variations in cognitive mode at the individual level might play out at the cultural level. In particular, I was thinking of the vast differences between the Eastern and Western worlds. The pervasive differences in cultural norms, in religion, philosophy, science, arts, language, and even writing systems, may just stem from a very basic difference in the extent to which the analytic mode was established in different areas of the world. I had hoped to find other experimental research on that subject, similar to Bruce Dunn's work (Chapter 5). Even though the analytic/holistic differences are accepted ideas in psychology, I could find no further works exploring the implications for any other aspects in human thought and interaction. In fact, I *found very little psychological research on the East/West dichotomy in general, so I set aside my thoughts on this question.*

Then, a few years back, I was looking through a pile of books on semiotics that had been set aside for later reading. Within the collection, I found a work by Floyd Merrell from 2002, entitled, Learning Living, Living Learning: Signs between East and West. *In this volume Merrell was presenting a very thorough look at the commonalities between Buddhist ideas on knowledge and his take on Peircean sign theory. The coincidence, in this case, was that I had yet again found information I was seeking within my own library. As it happens, Floyd Merrell's work was prompted by similar life experience, as he points out that he didn't go looking for connections, they just appeared in the course of life:* "One simply has to open one's eyes and look, really look—as if holding William Blake's grain of sand in your hand were the key to the universe's secrets" (Merrell 2002, 3). *My initial response to this find was not to venture into this new direction in my academic work (though we do touch upon these ideas about East versus West later in this chapter) but to finally begin to see what I have reported on throughout my story, the serendipity behind discovery. My first look at Merrell's book was for me a true "aha" moment, an epiphany that led me to begin, finally, to appreciate fully the gifts of happenstance that had guided my work. This is particularly ironic in that I was fully aware of the importance of coincidences in one's life and, in fact, had been building a record of them for years.*

Being anthropologists who were thoroughly familiar with the gamut of religious belief systems of the world, we found that choosing one particular tradition over another was a limiting element for our daughter's education. Terry tended to embrace a wide range of religious ideas, while I tended to eschew them all. In the foundational ideas of animism, however, we found common ground. Hence, we set our life philosophy in this direction as the guiding principle in our daughter's upbringing. In the ensuing years there were surprising, and sometimes significant, events in our experience that seemed to reinforce our decision. We call these events "spiritual confirmations." After years of successive instances of such confirmation, we began to record them in a journal, whether they seemed truly momentous or merely odd coincidences.

For reasons that I still don't understand, my finding the book on Eastern thought in semiotics gave me the push to see at last how serendipity had shaped the whole direction of our work on language origins. As anthropologists, the personal and academic areas of life had to be closely related anyway, for those who seek to understand humanity seem always to look "within" as well as "without." Once I had acknowledged the many confirmations supporting our semiotic view of human evolution, it was clear that our book should include personal experience within the telling of the argument. The organization for this volume, then, became clear. We have presented the whole of our argument in the preceding chapters. This chapter, then, offers some discussion of what language as a modeling system gave to our species, as well as a less-technical recapitulation of the archeological sequence with a specific eye toward the emergence of humanity as we are now.

TIME AND THE SIGN

The concept of "time" in most languages overflows with meaning. But, unlike many products of human symbol production that take on a wide range of connotations, the importance of time does not lie simply in the significance laid on it by people. Time is elemental to existence. According to physicists, for example, everything is in motion, and movement is defined as a measure of distance in space over a specific unit of time. It is the inherent connection between space and time that results in the notions that time might actually be altered, or warped, by the compression of matter through gravitational forces and possibly even contained in black holes (Gribbin 1992, 28–57).

Time is also inherent to our physical selves. We have several internal clocks that influence our biological schedule and our perceptions of time (Wright 2002). We use a perceptual "interval timer" to help us judge how long particular immediate events may last. This is what gives us a sense of rhythm for music and what allows the coordination of other more basic endeavors such as the timing of movement to catch a ball, maneuvering a car through traffic, or any locomotion for that matter. Then there is the circadian clock, which serves to coordinate sleep cycles with the Earth's daily cycles. It also regulates daily fluctuations in body temperature, blood pressure, and hormonal secretions. Unlike the interval timer, which may be subject to conscious control and is highly inaccurate, the circadian rhythms are inflexible schedules that do not tend to vary widely despite environmental fluctuations. The circadian cycles are not simply controlled through neural activity but are actually part of the genetic makeup of organs and tissues, with varying cycles that respond to other external cues, such as eating schedules that affect the timing of liver function. Finally, there is the internal clock that determines the overall length of one's life—one that can limit life span even in the absence of disease or tragic external events. This form of physiological clock is still not well understood, but it may relate to the mitotic clock, which limits mitosis in individual cells.

Dimensions of time, external and internal, are simply part of our existence despite our level of awareness about them. Like much of the automated aspects of the central nervous system, the biological clocks work largely outside the realm of conscious thought. And the "time" that is integral to the physical universe is, of course, independent of our notice. But "time" as a conceptual entity, as a rhematic symbol, is a product of our awareness. We contend that this awareness of time became emphasized within *Homo sapiens* in concurrent development with the dominantly analytic mind of the fully linguistic animal—with the dawn of anthroposemiosis.

There are numerous direct examples of symbolic notation of time in the archaeological evidence, including a few from the late Upper Paleolithic and Mesolithic of France and Spain (Marshack 1991, 81–108). Additionally, a few possible Paleolithic "moon records" or other examples of "time-factored thought" (see Marshack 1972, 1991, 109–24; see also Rudgley, 1999, 92–99; Von Petzinger 2017, 236–42) suggest that the nascent reorganization of experiential patterns into recurrent symbolic representation was at least founded by the people of the Mesolithic era, well before the explosion of Neolithic cultures.

Remember what we have established about the aspects of analytical thinking that seems to be relevant to the evolutionary trend in the hominid line. First, the analytical thinker takes the perceptions of the senses and alters the data in several ways, rather than storing them as a more directly iconic representation. The sensory input is broken down, segmented, and organized into salient items of information. Detail of recall is reduced, but certain elements of the environment are considered more worthy of note, as nodes of relevant data. This segmentation allows, then, a second tier of information manipulation—a process of interconnecting the nodes within memory that results in the construction of generalized concepts, logical types, and novel constructs. Concepts are then abstracted in a codified manner, a mental shorthand. We use the word "shorthand" to highlight the efficiency that this mode of thought must engender, the ability to coordinate experiences from radically diverse situations into new appreciations of the world.

Pattern recognition, essentially iconic signification, is what determines the salient elements to be stressed and codified. Connections provide the propositional inferences to solve immediate problems within one's activities of the present. But alterations between successive experiences also point to patterns in time. Some elements of pattern recognition exist among all animals, working at the iconic and indexical level. These forms of signs are involved in discernment of *changes* in the environment, in territorial familiarity, in the status of the surrounding plant and animal life, the changes and recurrence in temperature, and many other environmental variations. However, the movement of features in the sky, connected to the anticipation of seasonal patterns, is a more propositional (or dicent) element in pattern recognition, and though these phenomena may be individually experienced iconically, connecting them in meaningful ways symbolically must occur through an unfolding correlation of past information.

In language as a modeling system, such correlation is essentially founded by the emergence of temporal elements of syntax. The large-scale experience of such patterns, internalized as symbolic systems of correlation, represents a profound advance over mere iconic apprehension of sign objects in the surrounding world. Thus, monthly (lunar) and yearly (solar) cycles can be consciously recognized only by an animal with a capacity for higher orders of symbolling (dicent symbols coordinated into arguments). Once a pattern of "growth in plants over time" becomes consciously evident through the correlation of independent "bubbles" of thought, then there exists the possibility for inspiring manipulation of that growth. Let us consider what the archaeological record suggests about this process after the Paleolithic era.

THE COGNITIVE IMPLICATIONS OF THE MESOLITHIC

Analytical dominance, as illustrated by the archaeological record, indicates a mind capable of setting up relational connections that transfer across events. Significant features of data in memory are connected not just within an event, but as a conscious appreciation of events from episode to episode in a linear fashion, as a time line from past to future, real awareness of the results of change through time. This engenders the creation of the story of our individual histories, our personal narratives and the invention of narrative in general. Analytical thought ushers in an era of complex mythmaking, empirical learning, and the development of rule-based behavior, such as the inherently learned phonological and grammatical system that constitutes language as communication (Haworth and Prewitt 2010). The increasing dependence upon analytical thought in *Homo sapiens* is the beginning of time consciousness—the discovery of time.

We have placed strong emphasis on the Mesolithic era as a time when, within groups and across the whole Old World, at least, the primary capacities of holistic thought were steadily augmented by locally variable enhanced analytical capacities. This cognitive platform shift, occurring over some ten thousand years (twenty-five thousand to fifteen thousand years ago), moves human prehistory from a long-established stone-tool tradition, through a radical development of new tool forms, and finally into intensive technological manipulation of the environment that we associate with the Neolithic. The transition begins with the exceptional mobiliary and parietal art of the Upper Paleolithic, sharing more with the earlier technologies of the Lower and Middle Paleolithic (Mellars 1994, 42–78), but ends with a plethora of local and regional cultures engaged in worldwide expansion through cultural adaptation. Within the Mesolithic there are no strong skeletal clues about the cognitive evolution that was taking place, as there were with earlier species of hominids. But we argue that the adjustments of life span, nervous system ontogeny, group dynamics and mating, and elaboration of technology worked together as limits and pressures favoring first emphasis on immediate sharing of analytical insights between individuals, and then the group establishment of modeling systems that enhanced survival (cultures). In other writing we referred to the changes as moving from Language I (rhematic and propositional systems) to Language II (modeling systems grounded in the symbolic argument) (see Haworth 2006; Haworth and Prewitt 2010).

In terms of the archaeological record, the Mesolithic represents a culmination in lithic tool technology with the appearance of microlith industries (Mithen 1994, 96) and other material elaborations. The sites also provide evidence for structures, at least semi-regular settlement, the first cemeteries, and burials with grave goods, and with these elements likely came the establishment of the earliest kinship categories (see also Mithen 1994, 79–135). The range of variability in the archaeological record of the Mesolithic led Steven Mithen (1994, 133–35) to characterize the period as being a finale to the hunter-gather era and a prelude to the economic systems of later prehistory.

Our supposition, and we must emphasize that this is complete supposition, is that biologically, through natural selection and gene flow, there was a continuous re-fitting of neuronal bundles and connections of the brain to accommodate the material and behavioral changes during the Mesolithic period. That is, we believe the Mesolithic represents a critical juncture in the cognitive evolution of our species: establishment or reinforcement of neural connections that were not strongly represented before about twenty thousand years ago, but were fully established by at least fifteen thousand years ago in most areas of the world. We recognize that within language-origins studies this is a radical biological hypothesis. Even so, it is not inconsistent with a punctuated-equilibrium model for the Hominidae.

We also emphasize that the holistic mind has not disappeared from human cognition, in general or in individuals, but rather that its role was diminished by the emphasis of technological and behavioral changes at a critical evolutionary transformation. This accounts for why the many individuals within Upper Paleolithic populations capable of producing what we regard as extraordinary artistic achievements are contrasted during the Mesolithic record with artists whose representations are more stylistically abstract (Mellars 1994, 78; Haworth 2007). Indeed, in human populations today, stylistic abstractions are still primary at a very young age (Mithen 1994, 127–32; Haworth 2007), except among a few holistic-dominant thinkers and individuals who are trained in realistic modes of representation. As we have seen, the rock art of the Spanish Levant presents a unique illustration of this continued progression in art.

By the end of the Mesolithic, we can comfortably posit a world suffused with symbolic arguments—stories, myths, explanations, religious systems, kinship systems, and explicit systems of technological development and application. These are the trappings of a time-conscious species. We must re-emphasize that something like the Mesolithic was extant worldwide before the expansion of derived Old World populations into the New World about fourteen thousand years ago. What follows essentially "Mesolithic" patterns, worldwide, has always struck anthropologists as a truly spectacular florescence of local traditions, populations, and technologies. So, we now turn to the impacts of the human Mesolithic transformation, the Neolithic systems of adaptation to new environments, the success of *Homo sapiens* manifest in population growth, and the foundations of tribal organization, chiefdoms, and civilization.

THE NEOLITHIC AS THE CULMINATION OF THE MESOLITHIC TRANSFORMATION

The semiotic appreciation of "time"—that is, human reflections upon the experience of time—strikes us as the most important outcome of the emergence of language as a modeling system. Indeed, without the advent of time modeling, the domestication of plants and animals, one of the primary defining characteristics of the Neolithic era, could never have occurred. Thus, while the Mesolithic offers a strong indication of our species becoming fully anthroposemiosic and manipulating local environments to advantage, it is in developments following the Mesolithic that we see the real impacts of these new capacities.

The Neolithic Age emerges as an accelerating shift in human material culture, producing (1) rapid worldwide expansion of humans into new environments; (2) an emphasis and elaboration of compound tool forms; (3) the origins of horticulture and agriculture and their concomitant tendencies toward sedentary communities; (4) the appearance of village culture and ultimately cities; (5) the invention of writing in different key areas of the world; (6) the elaboration of social elites in complex kin-based social structures; (7) more complex systems of burial for the dead attesting symbolic beliefs about life and death; (8) the foundations of oral tradition involving projection of "life" onto animistic and then zoomorphic or anthropomorphic gods, often seen as ancestors or creators in territorial associations of politically organized societies; and (9) organized conflict within and between distinct groups. Except where otherwise cited, for a general view of these developments relating to the following discussions, see Fagan and Durrani (2016).

What anthropologists call "Neolithic," indeed, continued in cultural practices well into the historical period, including a few areas outside the impact of civilization within the past two centuries. There can be little doubt that within the developments from Lower, Middle, and Upper Paleolithic cultures through Mesolithic cultures, a few of these elements were nascent, but with the Neolithic we are presented with whole populations who are essentially human in the same sense as any current member of our species. In other terms, we were "skeletally" human long before we became fully "biologically" human, for the continuing adjustments in brain structure and cognitive applications to the surrounding world, operating over the past 150,000 years at least, brought humanity into its current state. And within that evolution, the appearance of the symbolic argument, among other developments involving symbolling, is most signaled archaeologically by the cultures of Neolithic peoples.

The studies of Neolithic culture present a vast record, well documented in many core areas, and generally complete across most of the world. Though the timing of what may be called Neolithic advances varies widely in different regions, the general florescence of Neolithic culture is apparent as a worldwide development. We do not attempt any full synthesis of the period, but instead are presenting ideas relating to how Neolithic culture, as anthropology understands it, fits within our argument on the timing of the origins of language as a full-blown mark of humanity as we experience it. Among the various evidences of language in human culture, we believe five adequately illustrate what is involved in the full emergence of what we might call *Homo sapiens* loquitur: (1) technology, (2) horticulture and agriculture, (3) kinship, (4) oral narrative, and (5) writing.

Technology

We know that textiles and pottery both have a long history, reaching back to the Mesolithic. Because of the durability of fired clay, the lack of pottery in most Mesolithic contexts suggests that ceramics were mainly an elaboration of human activity during the Neolithic, and indeed well into that time period. Most archaeologists consider ceramics a firm mark of Neolithic status, regardless of how early pottery occurs. Pottery also often shows decoration and textures in the form of cord impressions, attesting to complex practices of cord production from various fibers. Textiles present a rather different potential, and basketry even more so, given the evidence of nets and bark containers at very early dates. However, archaeologists have tended to see all of these innovations as foundational to the Neolithic.

Stone tools of the Mesolithic do show a marked change from the assemblages of the Paleolithic, with small blades and laminar microliths becoming prominent at the end of the Paleolithic and early Mesolithic, indicating the appearance of compound tool production. The geometric microliths used in compound tools during the later Mesolithic continued in Neolithic cultures, especially those focused mainly on hunting. Hunting tools of the Neolithic included spears, knives, and arrows hafted to wood or bone with resins and cords or sinews. In addition to hunted animals, sheep and other herd animals were kept for meat and ultimately were integrated into use as domesticated draft animals. During the later Neolithic, with animal and plant domestication prominent in many areas of the Old World, stone technology associated with hunting was de-emphasized, but where it remained prominent, specialized and often stylized local or regional assemblages occurred, including points, knives, gravers, scrapers, grinding stones, incipient uses of metals, and decorative items.

While Mesolithic people buried their dead, the practice was without much elaboration. During the Neolithic, burial mounds, complicated systems of inhumation, cremation, preservation, and differential treatment of the dead became common. Burial mounds were constructed in many areas of the Old and New worlds, often involving substantial inclusion of artifacts and other grave goods. Burial systems provide the strongest information about social stratification, belief in some kind of life after death, decorative or aesthetic body modifications during life, and classes of tools that were seen as either utilitarian or signs of status. Because of the distinctive nature of these artifacts, we also see in the Neolithic clear indications of "tribal" and "regional" styles that mark out areas of widespread social interaction, religious systems, and economic activity.

All of these elaborations signal not only the independent development of many local and regional cultures, but also the *necessity of languages* to support such activity, with individual systems of linguistic communication no doubt rising from the immediate connections and needs of local groups. This is not to say that language might not have had, at earlier dates, some broad commonalities over wide areas, but the likelihood that language rose from a single source of phonological and lexical patterns is very small. Moreover, the occurrence of presumably logographic symbolic rhemes during the Paleolithic do not require a common spoken system. As we have noted earlier, people most likely developed "language as communication" as they found things in their experience worth sharing between individuals. We presume that such sharing was never universal for our species, but rose from the ground of indexical and iconic experience that gave humans adaptive advantages in the myriad environments they entered during their spread across the continents. Historical linguistics does not belie this premise, since the diversity within language families seems to arise from geographic expansion of particular, politically dominant systems within smaller geographic ranges. This is also not inconsistent with languages undergoing attrition as historical and modern systems have gained cycles of "advantage" through political dominance. The shifting alliances between widespread individual systems and local variants or outliers, we believe, represents an old tendency parallel to the material complexities that are well documented for the Neolithic Age.

Horticulture and Agriculture

The story of how intensive gathering of naturally occurring grains or root crops led to domestication in Mesopotamia, Mexico, China, and the Andes was well documented by twentieth-century archaeologists. The processes involved also appear incipiently in the Mississippi Valley of North America and in some of the specialized horticultural routines of Polynesia. We are also aware that intensive gathering of abundant food resources led to individual resource ownership and high population densities in what is now California, without domestication of those resources. But, in general, the later Neolithic involves not only the inception of agriculture, but its continental spread as farming populations grew. For the Old World, numerous authors have offered comprehensive theories of the diverse causes behind agricultural developments, stressing the close connections between demography, technological innovation, and acquisition of new crops and domestic animal resources.

Alongside technology and basic organization of cultivation, Neolithic peoples empirically attained requisite knowledge of seasons, growing cycles and development of seed varieties, and astronomical associations that enabled prediction of annual flooding or other elements important to water control. More than in perhaps any other area of culture, these developments make use of explicit time consciousness. But even in hunting and gathering cultures, knowledge of growing cycles for specialized localities within a region are important, relying both on a cognitive mapping of where resources might be located and the best seasons during which to exploit them. Thus, whether people were hunter/gatherers, nomadic pastoralists, or farmers, the annual cycle is an important part of cultural patterning. And some cycles involve long observations through time of the sort which must be shared across generations rather than being learned by individuals directly through observation. Without language, oral tradition, the organization of groups into generational hierarchies through kinship, and specific "instruction" within technological regimes, none of these developments of the Neolithic could have occurred.

Kinship

Perhaps the greatest achievements of modern anthropology have been in the realm of recording and classifying the many forms of kinship extant in the living ethnographic record. While the native Australians maintained a very basic "stone-age" material culture, their kinship systems were elaborated into some of the most complex symbolic adaptations of human existence. And though these systems may appear to be more complex than the structures of Near Eastern, African, Asian, or North American cultures, they may simply be "less derived" to accommodate elements such as class, caste, or other organizations of human social hierarchy. Moreover, Australian technology, though "stone-age" in many general ways, does not belie the point that Australian conceptual elaborations of kinship are essentially Neolithic in manifestation. The long historical tendency of human kinship reckoning, looking forward to the present day, in fact, seems to have been one from more-complex to less-complex forms of kinship address, rules of marriage, and reckoning of descent. At the same time, the long-term trend is toward greater social stratification and complexity in the system of production, and thus in social categories beyond basic kinship distinctions (Kaplan, Hooper, and Gurven 2009; McConvell 2018).

We know today that the complementarity underpinning the many Australian section systems provides examples of kin definitions relating to long-term environmental adaptations that possibly go back to Mesolithic origins. The most complex classifications such as the Murngin kin inventory and marriage rules apparently relate to richer natural resource areas with greater population density, versus the relatively simple versions of the basic four-section system (often identified with type descriptions of the Kariera system) from which adaptive elaborations may have sprung (see, for example, McConvell 2018, 1–20). Even so, there are no clear-cut correlations grounding all Australian social-structural variants to ecology, since historical traditions tend also to influence what terms a particular group might use. The key to these systems is "finding a proper mate" within the demographic spread of groups on the landscape, as well as forcing exogamy in the interest of widening a local group's network for resource access. In addition to this, the medium of what is permissible or not is very much based in looking beyond the living memory of the lineage, to the remote generations of past and future that also comprise "the group." Ultimately, kinship is always steeped in the appreciation of time, and in that context, constitutes a culturally specific semiotic argument.

Australian and similar kinship systems often venerate ancestors in totemic associations with animals. In later segmented kinship systems, ancestors may also become venerated or elevated to the status of chthonic beings, apical clan/sib ancestors, or deities. What is almost a bewildering accounting of subtleties to most modern Western people constituted a necessary elaboration of relationships essential to long-term survival of kin groups. It may be difficult for our Western consciousness to understand how one might commit "incest" by marrying a person from a far distant community with whom one might have difficulty tracing any specific genealogical tie, or not committing incest by marrying a relatively close cousin. Yet, traditional people handle the systems they are born into quite easily. For example, native Australians negotiated the symbolic terrain of kinship as easily as New Yorkers negotiate the subway schedule. All of which is to say, in all fully modern humans, language focuses on details that are important to cultural context. But such elaborated systems had to begin with certain basic labeling of relationships, reckoned from the "self" or "ego," and extending as far as necessary to other individuals, given the conditions of familiarity, subsistence, and necessary cooperation.

We may posit something like the historical kinship systems of Australia going back as far as the Mesolithic, if not the late Paleolithic, since "kin categories" within a group would necessarily have been an important early subject of rhematic symbolling. It should be noted that such systems became at least "propositional" as early regulators of mating preference or proscription. Beyond the Mesolithic, however, we see ample evidence of the kinds of social stratification and specialization relating to production and resource access, which would give rise to more "derived" systems. For example, the kinship principles of exogamy, endogamy, and larger systemic relations are found in the Torah Book of Genesis as grounds for tribal- and state-level hierarchy (see Prewitt 1990). Though presented in a written tradition, these concepts go well back into the oral stage of Neolithic culture. This system is also highly correlate with the Greek and other Indo-European systems we have encountered as derived from oral tradition in early written sources. Overall, in the area of kinship, the Neolithic certainly manifests cultures that would necessarily have employed relational arguments of the kinds we have encountered historically through documents and ethnography among tribes, chiefdoms, and primary state-level systems.

Oral Narrative

We have already noted that there are evidences of "narrative" in the rock art of the Spanish Levant. Narrative, of course, is strong evidence for propositional thinking, if not also for the emergence of the Peircean argument in human experience. What we read into images we encounter, however, may not be entirely what was involved in their creation. So, we should ask: What are the evidences of old oral traditions, or contemporary processes of storytelling that we might be able to project into the distant past? One immediate suggestion comes from John Marshall's 1957 film *The Hunters*, which tells the story of four !Kung hunters tracking and killing a giraffe in the Kalahari Desert. In one segment of the film, after the hunt, one of the hunters entertains the others in his group by telling the story of the exploit with words and gestures. Alongside many other examples, this "ethnographic" film captures the sense of the importance of the hunt in the lives of the !Kung people, underscoring the art of "telling" as a series of vignettes arranged to produce dramatic anticipation. Essentially, the storyteller relies upon extant "knowledge" of the world to provide a culturally meaningful experience for those who were not present on the hunt itself. The story is speech in context, relying on iconic and symbolic appreciation of the specific content as part of a pattern. In fact, the art of the Spanish Levant, when it presents as "narrative," has much the same quality, though presented in an array serving an immediate holistic interpretation. In the oral presentation, too, one works toward a final holistic outcome.

By stringing a series of speech or performative acts together, one works toward a completion, but that completion does not always have to be thought of as mere linear presentation. A Native American acquaintance who taught communication studies once expressed to us the idea that story narratives often work in the pattern of a wheel, with individual elements serving as spokes arranged around a non-stated hub. The same analogy may even apply to discussions concerning some possible action or intent, as with the gathering of men in the film *Dances with Wolves* who are trying to decide what to do about the soldier at the fort. The hub of the various arguments necessarily presented in a linear sequence but comprising disconnected thoughts will not, in the end, need statement, because the listener may deduce the "point" from the possible logical connections of the elements. The cultural assumption is that everyone "knows" enough to fill in information that is non-stated.

This is no different than any string of morphs in a sentence, working toward the "full stop" that makes the idea of the sentence complete. At the level of the "wheel" discourse, the sequence of phrases or sentences or longer statements moves toward another level of completion, a gestalt which is in fact a consensus manifestation of Peircean argument. What is important here is that "story" is a linear process serving the interests of some holistic appreciation that will, at some point, become evident. While we attend to sentences and discourses for such revelation unconsciously, we may also build into a story some repetitions of elements that remind one to "look back" or draw connections among elements that are not in direct linear sequence. This is precisely the intent and effect of the structure called chiasmus, or rhetorical inversion, that occurs in Torah scriptures (see Prewitt 1990), many ancient Greek texts, various forms of poetry, and some Renaissance literature. In Torah and ancient Greek writing, these features are also mnemonic elements that aid in processing long narratives orally. Thus, in the earliest written traditions of Western culture, alongside some of the Irish and Slavic oral traditions, the "wheel" analogy fits as a formal part of story development "around" some "completion" or conclusion. The holistic appreciation of the array of elements, while also aiding in mastering large bodies of symbolic presentation, has deep roots in the earliest known narratives, and presumably in the earliest manifestations of narrative in human culture.

It is on this basis that we see a connection of Mesolithic rock art depicting groups engaged in common activity, hunting or dancing scenes, as potential narrative. The recurrence of pattern, moreover, as we witness throughout folklore, ancient theater, and even in early Modern theater, is not far removed from a !Kung hunter recounting his experience. The "hearer" bears some responsibility for taking the body of elements presented to the level of a holistic result, and that is one of the ways the Peircean argument works as "symbol"—an arbitrary and conventional way of expressing some much more meaningful object in an unlimited semiosis, or perfusion of signs. The Mesolithic presents some tantalizing hints of such complex representation, but nothing definitive. However, when we piece together all the elements of the Neolithic archaeological record, there is nothing to refute the idea that full-blown discursive narrative is involved in every aspect of life, even in the absence of written records. *If people think in stories*, then Neolithic populations are people like us in every element of cognition and behavior.

Writing

The origin of writing is an element of human evolution we have not taken up strongly in developing this book. This is because everything we have suggested about the early use of symbolic rhemes applies equally to inscribed or spoken forms. In other terms, as soon as humans were capable of assigning arbitrary and conventional "meanings" to inscribed marks, we may presume that such assignments could also have been made to articulations of the sound stream. We consider such marks not to be secondary to the spoken use of symbols—that is, spoken and inscribed rhemes should be co-extant. With that understanding, we consider the recent catalog and analysis of Paleolithic written symbols in association with animal paintings to be an important addition to our knowledge of early human speech potentials (Von Petzinger 2017). Further, these capabilities in the area of inscribed symbolic rhemes have been suggested to go back to at least sixty thousand years ago in South Africa (Texier et al. 2013), and, as noted in Chapter 3, have dated in one European cave at sixty-five thousand years ago (Hoffmann and Standish et al. 2018). The overall record doesn't preclude the verbal symbolic dicent or argument from the Paleolithic human repertoire, but as we have suggested the argument in particular did not likely come as quickly as basic propositions. That is, as the ape language experiments have shown, just because a species has a capacity for symbolic rhemes, that doesn't mean that it will habitually conform its world to symbols.

Indeed, the creation of written symbolic dicents and arguments does not appear anywhere until about five thousand years ago, long after humans were showing diversity and specialization in every other area of material culture. The lag of writing behind the development of full-blown language is also shown in the poetic and other mnemonic devices of oral traditions generally, which also show up as artifacts of oral tradition in early narrative and philosophical texts of the Sumerians, Greeks, and Hebrews (see Prewitt 1990 for a discussion of such elements in Torah). In all of these examples, "knowledge" in the form of the symbolic argument represented the world through systems of belief. A shift to a more pragmatic view of nature—as alternative "explanations"—occurred for the Greeks, among others, as religious constructs moved in the direction of general philosophical inquiry. David Abram (1996) suggests that this "philosophical" transition occurred for the Greeks when they adopted an alphabet completely divorced from the animistic and iconic connections that remained for the people of the Near East who originated the characters. We do not completely agree with this assessment, given numerous counter examples, the diversity of early writing systems, and especially the sense in which iconic underpinnings of Chinese writing were ultimately adapted to a conventional symbolic/logographic system. In the case of oriental systems, indeed, the advantage of the evolution of writing was that the system of signs conveys parallel meanings for many different languages that do not share phonological, morphological, or syntactic systems. The disadvantage is the plethora of signs that must be internalized, as opposed to alphabetic systems that strategically target phonology. Thus, a Korean or Japanese person can more or less read Chinese texts with some level of understanding (though more recently these systems have continued to diverge). This is not quite the same as an English speaker who might be able to gloss some elements of texts from other Indo-European languages but cannot glean underlying meaning when encountering an alphabetic text from another language family.

For us, writing is just a more explicit example of a linear string of symbols serving a process in which, at some point, a gestalt is configured to bring into the foreground a whole apprehension—what we call today a sentence or phrase. But writing also provides an apparent concreteness to language that does not exist in speech. What is fluid and unconscious, and ephemeral in speech becomes renegotiated into a segmented medium, experienced as fixed signs whose interpretation exists in the moment, and across vast expanses of time. Thus, we use the Shakespeare folio to find hints of the spoken forms that prompted the text, while also providing diverse contemporary performative or critical "readings." We may understand the earliest Chinese writing, incised oracle inscriptions on bones, as essentially dicent symbolic inscriptions, while longer texts in Mesopotamia constituted written symbolic arguments. In the case of Mesopotamia, moreover, we now know that the written medium has a much older physical counterpart in the rhematic tokens used in trading goods over wide distances (Schmant-Besserat 1992). In Mesopotamia, we also see examples of dicent symbolic writing in the incision of iconic/symbolic elements on the clay envelopes that enclosed the tokens—a form of double-ledger accounting. Given the use of weaving in mnemonic devices in historical cultures of South America (Urton and Brezine 2005), we may also suggest that the two ancient innovations of pottery and weaving were instrumental in "material" symbolism running back to at least the late Neolithic.

All of this supports the interpretation we have presented in earlier chapters that the appearance of *spoken language* as we know it comprised a gradual and uneven process from the late Paleolithic through the Mesolithic, with symbolic thought preceding habitual speech, and with the Neolithic representing a more or less complete, worldwide, dominance of analytical-sequential processing in our modes of communication. In our view, we emphasize that writing, in spite of some very early precursors, does not become a critical element of human cultural evolution until the rise of civilizations. History tends to give emphasis to writing, and attempts to project the efficacy of a material component to language for modern people back into pre-literate periods. However, though the impact of writing on major cultural traditions should not be underestimated, we note that writing developed independently for different initial purposes.

Out of this broad view, there is still much to be learned about differences in the written systems that evolved in Asia, Mesopotamia, and the Americas. This incorporates the evolution of logographic symbols in Asia from early iconic forms, as well as the emergence of syllabary and alphabetic systems for writing speech sounds, also from early iconic representations (see Abram 1996). One implication of the differences extant today between Asian logographic systems and Western alphabetic systems is that holistic cognition may be more directly reinforced by the writing systems of oriental cultures. If that is true, then the balance of holistic versus analytic thinking may be more variable across human cultures than existing science has suggested.

WHAT THE NEOLITHIC IS, AND IS NOT

None of the foregoing is intended to say that language "emerged" exclusively or rapidly during the onset of the Neolithic. Nor do we believe language as we know it appeared full-blown as the result of some miraculous mutation or "cognitive awakening" in any period. Almost certainly, some elements of human symbolic communication were extant during the Mesolithic and Paleolithic. But the further we go back in time, the greater was the difference in how spoken communication was used, how many people within groups were adept in wielding symbols, and how important sharing ideas was to the overall survival of the group. We have tried to present a review of some salient features of the Neolithic that suggest fully derived language capabilities for groups and individuals. As many other researchers have suggested, it may be that the origins of human accomplishments are typically much earlier than when they are routinely manifest in the archaeological or historical record. Consistent with that idea, when we interpret the art and archaeology of the Neolithic as definitive of language, we still consider the Mesolithic to be rudimentary with respect to anthroposemiosis, so we stress that the use of a derived syntactic system seems unlikely to be the mainstay of Mesolithic groups.

The record of the Neolithic does help us understand why "language as communication" emerged and evolved in many different forms across the world, with conditions of cultural elaboration, the rise of dominant groups, population contact, mobility, and resource needs ultimately conferring prominence to some languages and essentially pruning away others. Humans have always likely had many local speech systems, and probably always will, as groups attempt to assert identity within the larger linguistic communities of which they are a part. Even today, for example, one may ask why African American Vernacular English and related dialects (in both black and white communities) continue to persist in the United States, while such dialects seem less prominent through time in some other societies. As much as a dialect may be stigmatizing in some ways, it may also stand as a protection against encroachment on identity from the outside. So, such variations, whether of languages within recognized historically connected families, full dialects, pidgins, or mere argots, always function in part for the adaptive continuity of some level of group. This, we suspect, is as old as the emergence of the first communicative language in ancient times.

CODA

"Finding" time provided the means to become, in evolutionary terms, a highly successful species. Our dominating population is ample proof of this. But it seems our extended cognitive realm may in the end still be too limited. We are still sufficiently shortsighted to put ourselves at risk. Despite lessons to be learned in ecology and biology, with myriad tales of a successful species invariably decimating the very environment that allowed that success, we are continuing to build our own population to troubling outcomes. Our history is filled with the evidence of our inability to foresee long-range repercussions to our ingenuity in all its forms. Our magnificent machines extend power beyond our physical limitations, but degrade the air. Our chemicals enhance our ability to produce food crops, but poison the water. The comfort of our shelters demands we devastate the world's forests.

While we hoped to offer a few potential solutions to some enigmatic questions from our past, we would also like to end with some encouragements for our future. We would like to encourage a concerted effort to open our collective mind to the elements of our population that do not fit with the ways of the dominating analytic cognitive mode. We are looking to fashion a mindset that is more attuned to the interconnectedness that is the hallmark of the holistic mode. Appreciating the whole as an entity that includes ourselves without separation from "the other" or "the external" may just be what is needed most at this point in time. The segmented values of the analytic thinker do not always provide the best answer.

In fact, we wonder if this has not been an unconscious problem throughout our history. There seems to be a deep-level longing underlying all the world's philosophies and religions that speaks to a sense of loss that accompanied our separation into a discrete "I." Could it be that the underlying reality of the ecstatic religious experience is a glimpse into a lost apprehension of the world through the purely holistic mode—apprehension of the world where one feels and intuits the close interconnection with everything outside us, the all?

This may be, however, a less problematic concept across the world's populations. The comparatively more holistic concepts underlying Asian culture, with its religious ideas of pluralism and more iconic writing systems, suggest a variation in the extent to which the analytic mode dominates within the spread of our species across the world. As Floyd Merrell notes (2002, 105):

> we in the West are by and large programmed to view ourselves as discrete, rugged individuals. We have individual bodies, individual minds, individual wills, individual talents, individual ideas and likes and dislikes. . . . Many non-Western societies tend to consider all forms of existence as making up a single universe. After all, the very word universe implies a united whole.

In fact, Merrell's book, mentioned earlier in this chapter, provides an extensive look at some basic quandaries set up in Western ideas about knowledge that can be easily and elegantly resolved through the basic aspects of Eastern philosophy. His insights in this realm appear to be understood through the application of one element of Western thought that is more in keeping with the "vagaries" of the Eastern concept of knowing, Peircean semiotics. His lesson on this begins with the following observation (62):

> Given the mind-boggling diversity the world presents to the confused onlooker, a set of fundamental premises was established prior to and during much of the seventeenth century and the Baroque period—itself a paragon of pluralism—for the purpose of laying conflicts regarding "reality" to rest for all time. Over the years, this set of premises became entrenched in the minds of us Westerners to the extent that they now color our world, the world we made.

Merrell goes on to discuss various dilemmas in Western thinking that center around a pervasive tendency to set up irresolvable dichotomies, beginning with Christianity's faith versus reason (2002, 62), but stemming largely from the mind/world "bifurcation" of Cartesian, Galilean, and Newtonian ideas (63–64). In Cartesian terms this was the dismissal of the *res extensa* (the subjective) in favor of *res cogitas* (the objective). The obvious successes of this mechanistic view of the last several hundred years tends to conceal the inherent difficulty with this separation, that no means of measurement of the "real" can be completely devoid of the subjective. There is simply no other means to experience the external, any external, whether it is the beauty of a rose or the numbered readout of a measuring device. Still, the relentless force of the scientific revolution served to suppress the occasional hint at the fallibility inherent in this idea of separation.

Merrell's volume proceeds to examine "knowing" as a means to illustrate our tenuous connections between our ideas of the world and its external reality. In essence, his lesson stresses the notion of the Eastern views that embrace the ineffable rather than strive against it. Also, as with our argument, Merrell found Peirce's concepts, including his sign categories, useful in explaining his thoughts on divergent ideas in Eastern and Western methods for understanding and knowledge. Primary in this overall argument is discovering the fallacies inherent in the segmentation, or bifurcation, of the Western method.

Our call here for greater recognition of the holistic thinkers in our midst, and for the holistic thought within ourselves, is to suggest a means for fulfilling a need in society and in us. We need to embrace *truths* like the underlying assumptions of a mathematical principle, as useful only as it applies for the particular problem at hand. We need to learn to be satisfied with the meaning here and now and to embrace and, more importantly, appreciate the constant unfolding of the signs upon signs that exist in and beyond the time of our lives.

WORKS CITED

Abram, David. 1996. *The Spell of the Sensuous*. New York: Vintage Books.

Dunn, Bruce R., Denise Dunn, David Andrews, and Marlin L. Languis. 1992. "Metacontrol: A Cognitive Model of Brain Functioning for Psychophysiological Study of Complex Learning." *Educational Psychologist* 27(4): 455–71.

Fagan, Brian, and Nadia Durrani. 2016. *People of the Earth: An Introduction to World Prehistory*. New York: Routledge.

Gribbin, John. 1992. *Unveiling the Edge of Time: Black Holes, White Holes, Wormholes*. New York: Three Rivers Press.

Haworth, Karen A. 2006. "Upper Paleolithic Art, Autism, and Cognitive Style: Implications for the Evolution of Language." *Semiotica* 162: 1/4, 127–74.

———. 2007. "Cognitive Style and Zoosemiotics." In *Semiotics 2004/2005*, edited by Stacy Monahan, Ben Smith, and Terry Prewitt. Ottawa: Legas Press.

Haworth, Karen A., and Terry Prewitt. 2010. "Two Steps toward Semiotic Capacity, Out of the Muddy Concept of Language." *Semiotica* 178: 1/4, 53–79.

Hoffmann, D. L., C. D. Standish, et al. 2018. "U-Th Dating of Carbonate Crusts Reveals Neandertal Origin of Iberian Cave Art." *Science* 359, no. 6378: 912–15.

Kaplan, Hillard S., Paul L. Hooper, and Michael Gurven. 2009. "The Evolutionary and Ecological Roots of Human Social Organization." *Philosophical Transactions of the Royal Society* B, 364 (1533) November. London: The Royal Society.

Marshack, Alexander. 1972. "Cognitive Aspects of Upper Paleolithic Engraving." *Current Anthropology* 13: 3/4, 445–77.

———. 1991. *The Roots of Civilization: The Cognitive Beginnings of Man's First Art, Symbol, and Notation* (Revised and expanded Second Edition). Mount Kisco, NY: Moyer Bell Limited.

———. 1992. "The Origin of Language: An Anthropological Approach." In *Language Origin: A Multidisciplinary Approach*, edited by J. Wind, B. Chiarelli, B. Bichakjian, A. Nocentini, and A. Jonker, vol 61, 421–48. *NATO ASI Series* (Series D: Behavioural and Social Sciences).

McConvell, Patrick. 2018. "Introduction: Revisiting Aboriginal Social Organization." In *Skin, Kin and Clan: The Dynamics of Social Categories in Indigenous Australia*, edited by Patrick McConvell, Piers Kelly, and Sébastien Lacrampe. Canberra: ANU Press, The Australian National University.

Mellars, Paul. 1994. "The Upper Paleolithic Revolution." In *The Oxford Illustrated Prehistory of Europe*, edited by Barry Cunliffe, 42–78. Oxford: Oxford University Press.

Merrell, Floyd. 2002. *Learning Living, Living Learning: Signs between East and West*. Toronto: Legas.

Mithen, Steven. 1994. "The Mesolithic Age." In *The Oxford Illustrated Prehistory of Europe*, edited by Barry Cunliffe, 79–135. Oxford: Oxford University Press.

Peirce, Charles S. 1867 [1984]. "On the Natural Classification of Arguments." In *Writings of Charles S. Peirce: A Chronological Edition, Volume 2, 1867–1871*, edited by Edward Moore et al., 23–48. Bloomington: Indiana University Press.

———. 1867a [1984]. "On a New List of Categories." In *Writings of Charles S. Peirce: A Chronological Edition, Volume 2, 1867–1871*, edited by Edward Moore et al., 49–59. Bloomington: Indiana University Press.

Prewitt, Terry J. 1990. *The Elusive Covenant: A Structural-Semiotic Reading of Genesis*. Bloomington: Indiana University Press.

Rudgley, Richard. 1999. *The Lost Civilizations of the Stone Age*. New York: The Free Press.

Schmant-Besserat, Denise. 1992. *Before Writing, Volume One: From Counting to Cuneiform*. Austin: University of Texas Press.

Texier, P-J, G. Porraz, J. Parkington, J-P Rigaud, C. Poggenpoel, and C. Tribolo. 2013. "The Context, Form and Significance of the MSA Engraved Ostrich Eggshell Collection from Diepkloof Rock Shelter, Western Cape, South Africa." *Journal of Archaeological Science* 40 (9): 3412–31.

Urton, Gary, and Carrie J. Brezine. 2005. "Khipu Accounting in Ancient Peru." *Science* 309 (5737): 1065–67.

Wright, Karen. 2002. "Times of Our Lives." *Scientific American* (September): 59–65.

Von Petzinger, Genevieve. 2017. *The First Signs: Unlocking the Mysteries of the World's Oldest Symbols*. New York: Simon & Schuster.

Index

Acheulean tools. *See* lithic technology
Africa, 3, 19, 26, 116, 117, 120, 121, 126, 141, 144
Aiello and Dunbar, 3, 24, 120
analytic thought, ix; as abstraction, 28, 46, 102–3; as balanced with holistic thought in Upper Paleolithic art, 52–54, 63, 125; defined, 2; as dominant over holistic thought, 1, 63, 70, 95–96, 105–8, 123–24; in experimental psychology, 58–61; as a key element in the evolution of language, 46, 71, 121–24, 126; as a limitation of research on holistic thought, 5, 61–63, 97–98, 103, 109–10; as linear or sequential processing, 4, 26, 46, 103–6, 146; as logical ordering and processing, 46, 122; as narrative, 46, 69, 106, 135; schematization of salient perceptions, 46–47, 102, 124; selection of qualities from holistic consciousness, 46, 102; time as an aspect of, 46, 107, 133–36; working in concert with holistic thought, 48, 148. *See also* cognition; Golding, William
anthroposemiosis, 78, 87, 90, 96–97, 109–10, 119, 126; as bubble logic, 106–10; as entailing the emergence of time awareness, 133, 147; as entailing logic and theorization, 82; as entailing the Peircean argument, 82; as grounded in pre-symbolic experience, 81; mythmaking capacity, 106–7, 135. *See also* semiosis
Antinucci, Francesco, 97–98
ape language experiments, 13, 17–18, 87–89, 96–98, 124, 144. *See* hominoids
argument, symbolic, 15–17, 79, 82, 126, 145–46; in association with the Neolithic, 138, 141; as built upon rhematic and dicent signs, 82, 87; as culture, 72; as distinctive of *Homo sapiens sapiens*, 90–91; as entailing iconic and indexical signs, 16–17, 82–83, 87; in habitual use of speech, 124, 126, 136; Peircean, 142–44; as potential in the Upper Paleolithic, 28–29; significance of narrative in, 46, 135. *See sign* classification third trichotomy
archaeological types as signs, 18, 84–85. *See also* signs
art: aesthetic maturity, 32, 126; of autistic savants, 31–33, 43, 45, 123; and emergent analytic mind,

69; holistic aesthetics, 121–22; normative childhood drawing, 31–32; Upper Paleolithic, 28, 51–54, 105–6, 122. *See also* cave art

Asia, 3, 25, 26, 27, 84, 123, 126, 141, 146, 148

Aurignacian tools. *See* lithic technology; Upper Paleolithic

Australia, 3, 26, 140–42

Australopithecus. *See* Hominids

autism, 31–39; Asperger's syndrome, 45; challenges of, 34–35, 41–42; eidetic memory in, 38, 42, 99; fragmented perceptions, 36; holistic dominance, 45–46; iconic bridges to concepts, 32–33, 42; late speech development, 31, 33, 35–36, 42–43; learning social conventions, 44; savant syndromes, 36–38, 43–44, 47, 98, 100, 123–24; self-reporting on, 34–35, 43–44; synesthesia, 44; variations in developmental process, 34–35, 43. *See also* art

Beltrán, Antonio, 67–71, 108

Binford, Lewis, 25

bipedalism, 116–20, 125; fetal-maternal incompatibility at birth, 117–18

Bordes, François, 25, 27, 84, 89

brain: Broca's and Wernicke's areas of, 119; exaptation of visual capacities for speech, 124; mutations relevant to human brain development, 71–72, 106, 147; neuronal specializations in, 19, 118–19; punctuated equilibrium in evolution of, 71–72, 120, 125, 136; size increases as a general Primate characteristic, 24, 88, 95, 116–17; size increase as a result of bipedalism, 117; stimulus-rich postnatal development in hominids, 58, 118; structures supporting cognition, 71–72, 97, 138

Brantingham, Kuhn, and Kerry, 3, 25–27, 50, 84, 88, 123

bubble analogy, 95–110. *See also* cognition; evolutionary process; language

cave art, 27–28, 67–68, 71, 105; abstraction versus realism, 28, 53; Altamira cave, 28, 51; Chauvet cave, 28, 52; dating of, 52; hand outlines, 28; as interpreted through analytic biases in scholarship, 63; Lascaux cave, 28, 49, 51; Niaux, 51; and other archeological manifestations, 54, 144; overlapping images in, 28, 50; symbolic elements, 29, 50, 121–24. *See also* art

Châtelperronian. *See* lithic technology

Chomyn, Nadia, 7, 31–34, 45, 48, 50, 52; maturity of representations, 32; overlapping images of, 32, 50; process over product, 32. *See also* art

Clark, W. E. Le Gros, 118–19

cognition, ix, x, 2–3, 19, 35, 79, 121, 144–46; animal, 45, 63, 81–82, 86, 96–97; holistic versus analytic, 2, 28, 43, 46, 63, 72, 104–7, 108–9, 136; linguistic biases in research, 8; metacontrol in, 58–61; normative biases in the social sciences, 33, 63, 98; styles, 41–48, 57–64

cognitive styles. *See* cognition

communication. *See* language

consciousness, ix–x, 1, 20, 63, 69, 101, 104, 107, 125–26, 135, 140–41

culture, x, 5, 26, 26, 28, 43, 46, 50, 67, 70–73, 87, 102, 107–8, 124–25, 134–46, 148; as a manifestation of the argument, 126

Cunliffe, Barry, 3, 24, 50, 67, 89, 105, 120

Deely, John N., v, 12–14, 124; on anthroposemiosis, 82

Derrida, Jacques, 78

Dibble, Harold, 18, 25

dicent or dicisign, 15–17, 26, 29, 46, 79, 81–82, 89–91, 96, 105, 121, 123, 126, 134–35, 144–46; as propositions, 82, 86–87. *See also* sign classification third trichotomy

Donald, Merlin, 24, 50, 101, 104

Dunn, Bruce, v, 8, 13, 57–64, 74, 108, 131; analytic and holistic modes as complementary continua, 58, 60; metacontrol in cognition, 58, 60

episodic memory, 101; as limiting foundational analytic thinking, 104

Europe, 3, 25–28, 50–51, 53, 84, 88, 105, 108, 120–21, 123, 126, 142, 144–45

evolutionary process: in Middle and Upper Paleolithic populations, 27, 121; neoteny as generative of culture in the genus Homo, 119; staged process of early hominid cognitive elaboration, 121; suggested by the art of the Spanish Levant, 71–72; synopsis of a semiotic view of evolution of hominid symbolling, 125–26; viewed through the bubble analogy, 101, 103–8. *See also* brain

Fitch, W. Tecumseh: synthetic research on cognition and stages in language development, 124

flint knapping, 77, 80–81, 84–85, 88. *See also* lithic technology

Fossey, Dian, 96

Fouts, Roger, 12, 13, 96, 118–20

Gazzaniga, Michael, 106–9

Golding, William, 103, 127n5

Goodall, Jane, 13, 96, 120

Gould, Stephen J., 50–52, 54, 124

Grandin, Temple, 34, 37, 39, 41–48, 63, 96, 98–100

Haworth, Karen A., 6–8, 23, 31, 33–34, 37, 39, 41, 48–49, 57–58, 64, 67, 73–74, 95, 131–32

holistic thought, 1, 54, 62, 106, 135; defined, 2; described as visual thinking, 41, 43, 45–46, 99; in experimental psychology, 58; as fundamental in human cognition, 63; as perception in general, 98–99; as shared broadly with other species, 63, 98; versus analytic, 59–60, 102. *See* cognition

Holocene, 3, 19

hominids, x, 3, 4, 13, 17–20, 23, 63, 72, 85, 87–88, 90, 103, 105, 118–20, 134–36; *Australopithecus*, 13, 19, 116–18; large and small bodied forms, 116–17; two-stage evolution of brain structure in, 120, 125; upright posture as a primary functional complex, 116–17. *See also* Homo

Hominoid: Bonobo, 15, 17, 86, 88; Chimpanzee, 7, 12, 14–15, 17, 88, 91, 116–20; *Dryopithecus*, 19; Gorilla, 17, 45, 88, 97, 100–101, 117–18; iconicity and indexicality among, 29, 86–87; motor ability at birth of, 58–59, 116; Orangutan, 17, 88; postnatal care in, 120; use of symbols, 17, 87, 90–91. *See also* ontogeny

Homo, 19, 33, 27–29, 104, 116–18, 125; archaic versus fully modern, 23–26, 35, 89; *erectus*, 3, 88, 91, 120–21; *ergaster*, 127n2; *habilis*, 118, 120, 127n2; *sapiens sapiens*, 2–3, 7, 23–29, 53, 72, 87, 90, 96, 103, 105, 108, 120–24, 133, 135, 137; *sapiens neanderthalinsis*, 24, 27, 84, 88–89, 91, 95, 120–21, 123

human paleontology, 3, 23, 24; paucity of tool/fossil associations, 19

human semiosis. *See* anthroposemiosis

icon, x, 18, 28–29, 46, 50, 52–54, 69, 71, 73, 79–90, 99, 102, 104, 121, 126, 134, 139, 143, 145–46,

148; defined, 15; iconic realism in Upper Paleolithic cave art, 28; as proposition, 17. *See also* sign classification second trichotomy
index, x, 16–18, 29, 46, 79–83, 85, 87–90, 102, 104, 121, 122, 125–26, 134, 139; defined, 15; as pre-symbolic calls, 81, 86; as proposition, 17; as symptoms in medicine, 15. *See also* sign classification second trichotomy
innenwelt, 90, 125
intelligence, 61, 71; animal, 45; IQ tests, 47; mapping of human measures onto other animals, 97; Piaget's stages derived from human ontogeny, 97–98; in popular science, 98
interpretant, 14, 82; defined, 79; as meaning in the here and now, 17, 79. *See also* sign classification

Köhler, Wolfgang, 96, 102
Kuhn, Steven, 25, 89, 121

Lacan, Jacques, 78
language: alphabetic and logographic writing, 145; ape language experiments, 16–18, 87, 98, 120, 124, 144–45; based in analytic or sequential cognition, 2, 62; in common usage, 96–97; as a communication system, 20, 23, 62, 81–83, 85, 120, 126, 135, 139, 147; as correspondence to the world, 87; as culture, 72–73, 125, 139–42, 147; defined, 11–20, 125; as defining the human species, ix, 1, 17, 72–73, 138; developmental process, 44; duality of patterning, 124; and kinship categories, 140–41; as a modelling system, x, 17–20, 24, 28–29, 96, 107, 109, 126, 132, 135–37; related to *umwelt* and *lebenswelt*, 119, 125–26; relevance of Peircean sign categories, 3, 81–83, 136; relevance to semiotic argument, 72–73; as a rule-based system, 17, 46, 107, 135–36; serving iconic and indexical interests, 86; as a shorthand for mental imagery, 33; syntax as a manifestation of time modeling, 133–35; theories of co-evolution with lithic technology, 72, 88–91, 121–22; and universal grammar, 46; varied development in autism, 31, 35–36, 42, 44, 47, 124; and writing, 145–46
lebenswelt, 14, 119, 124–26
legisign, 16, 46, 79–88, 102; defined, 14. *See also* sign classification first trichotomy
Levant region of the Near East, 27
Lilly, John C., 96
linear processing, 26, 143. *See also* analytic thought
lithic technology: Acheulean, 18, 88, 121–22, 125–26; Aurignacian, 24–25, 27, 123–25; blade industries, 24–25, 28, 105; Châtelperronian, 27, 123; flint knapping as experimental analysis, 77–79; form and function in, 84–85, 89, 121; indexicality as an important element of, 81, 85, 89; Magdalenian, 123–24; microliths of the Mesolithic, 107, 136; Mousterian, 18, 25, 88–89, 121–22; and Peircean sign typology, 84; as pre-symbolic pattern recognition, 85; as propositional, 88–89, 122; reduction stages versus designed forms, 25, 85, 91; reduction stages as syntax, 122; requisites for evidence of the symbolic argument, 89, 91; in sense and perception, 80; and sign processes, 26–26, 86–90; Solutrean, 18; in South Africa, 3; theories of co-evolution with communication, 72, 121. *See also* Lower Paleolithic; Middle Paleolithic; Upper Paleolithic
Lower Paleolithic, 84, 120–21

Magdalenian. *See* lithic technology
Mellars, Paul, 105–6, 108, 135–36
Merrell, Floyd, 13, 78, 132; Eastern versus Western thought, 148–49
Mesolithic, ix, 67–73, 95, 108, 123, 125, 134–39, 141–42, 144, 146; as central to the emergence of language, 73, 107, 136, 146–47; and compound tools, 107, 138–39; rhematic symbols in, 69. *See also* lithic technology; rock art of the Spanish Levant
messy text, 5
Middle Paleolithic, 27, 84, 120; analytical consciousness reflected in, 122, 125; archaeological types as pattern semiosis, 18, 25, 84; linear decision-making processes, 89; rhematic symbols in, 53–54; sub-species of Homo in cladistic association, 120–21; transition to Upper Paleolithic, 25–27, 123, 136
Mithen, Steven, 107–8, 122–23, 136
Mousterian, 18, 25, 84, 88, 122; dicent symbols in, 89; rhematic symbols in, 89, 121–22, 126. *See also* lithic technology; Middle Paleolithic

Nadia. *See* Chomyn
narrative, x, 28, 87, 91, 121; as central to human culture, 4–5, 20, 138, 142–45; in Mesolithic culture, 69–70, 135; and neural evolution, 71; as prominent in analytic thinking, 46, 71, 106–7, 126; in scientific discourse, 5
Neanderthal. *See* Homo
Neolithic, 68, 70–71, 95, 108, 123, 134–35, 137; horticulture and agriculture, 140; key characteristics of, 137; kinship, 140–42; oral narrative, 142–44; technology, 138–40; writing, 144–48. *See also* argument
neoteny, 118–19; as impetus to the emergence of culture, 119. *See also* evolutionary process; ontogeny

object, 15, 79–82, 84–86, 88, 134, 144; defined, 14. *See also* sign classification
ontogeny, 3, 58–59, 118–20, 135–36; comparisons among Hominoidea, 58–59; as expressed in autism, 35; as life span, 19; myelination, 35, 59, 118; neurogenesis, 58; stages of brain development, 97–98, 34–35; synaptogenesis, 35, 58, 118; synaptic decline, 58; variations in neuronal growth among hominoids, 117–20. *See also* evolutionary process; time

paradigmatic meaning, 78, 92n2
Peirce, C. S., x, 3, 8, 12–17, 74, 78–79, 96, 105, 107, 142–44, 149; perfusion of signs, 61, 78, 144; sign processes, x, 14, 24, 26, 79, 90; and stone technology, 84–91; ten sign types, 79–83, 110; triadic schema, 14–18. *See also* sign classification
Pfeiffer, John, 24, 50–51, 53, 67, 71
Pike, Kenneth, 12, 77
Pleistocene, 3, 19, 116–17, 125, 127n2
Pliocene, 3, 19
Prewitt, Terry J., 12–13, 74, 77–78, 115–16
Prince-Hughes, Dawn, 34, 46, 98–101

qualisign, 79–80, 82–84, 87, 89, 96; defined, 14. *See also* sign classification first trichotomy

representamen, 14, 82; defined, 79. *See also* sign classification
rheme, 15–17, 26, 29, 46, 50, 53–54, 79, 81–82, 85–91, 96, 102, 121–24, 126, 136, 139, 142, 144–46; defined, 15–16. *See also* sign classification third trichotomy
rock art of the Spanish Levant, 28, 67–73, 108, 136, 142–44; ambiguities in dating, 67, 69;

emotive representations in, 69, 71; human figures, 68–69, 71; as indicative of biological changes in cognition, 69; and narrative, 68–69; schematic representations in, 69; symbolic elements in, 69; typology of images, 68–69. *See also* art

Sacks, Oliver, 34, 37–39, 44, 46
de Saussure, Ferdinand, 8, 77–78; as ground for Lacan, and Derrida, 78; langue and parole, 78; semiotic limitations of, 78
Savage-Rumbaugh, Sue, 13, 86, 96, 120
Sebeok, Thomas A., 12–13, 88, 96
Selfe, Lorna, 31–33, 38, 103
semiosis: anthroposemiosis and semiotic capacity, 78–79, 120; as bases of species behavior, 14–15, 87, 89–91, 97; definition of, 14, 24; emergence of the capacity for the symbolic argument, 28; of flint napping, 84–85; as pattern recognition and propositional expression, 18, 26, 85; semiotic descriptions of specific models of semiosis, 83, 97, 103–6; as unconscious capacities, 14, 47; unlimited, 61, 78, 144. *See also* anthroposemiosis; zoosemiosis
Shreeve, J., 3, 24
signs: in animal behavior, 13, 17–18, 79, 86–87; as basis of life forms, 13–14; defined, 14; in lithic analysis, 26–27, 80, 84–85, 88–89; and mental constructs, 73, 87; and pragmatic meaning, 78; as preverbal phenomena, 35, 46, 79–80, 85; sense and perception, 15–16, 79, 145; token and type, 79; as a visualization of sign process in cognition, 88–90. *See* semiosis; sign classification
sign classification, x, 2–3, 13–14, 78–79, 80–83, 86–87, 96, 149; first trichotomy as relation to the form of the sign itself, 14, 79; second trichotomy as relation of representamen to object, 15, 79–81; third trichotomy as relation of representamen to interpretant, 15–16, 79, 81–82; ten sign categories expressed through three trichotomies, 14–18. *See also* lithic technology
sinsign, 16, 46, 79–80, 82–87, 102, 104; defined, 14. *See also* sign classification first trichotomy
Solutrean. *See* lithic technology
Spanish Levant. *See* rock art
speech, 4, 24, 29, 35, 43, 46, 73, 80, 86–87, 126, 143–44; as an extension of anthroposemiosis, 81; versus habitual symbolling, 89, 124
stone-tools, 3, 24, 26, 52–53, 103, 105–7, 122–23, 135, 138–39; as entailing signs, 19–20, 80, 84–91. *See* lithic technology
symbol, x, 14–20, 24–29, 32, 46, 50, 53, 68–70, 72–73, 79–83, 85–91, 96–97, 105–6, 117, 119–26, 133–47; as built upon icons and indices, 16, 18, 29, 73, 77, 86; as distinguished by convention, 15–16; malleability of meaning, 17. *See also* sign classification second trichotomy
symbolling, 17, 29, 72; habitual, as indicative of the emergent argument, 18, 29, 81, 88, 91, 123–24
syntagmatic meaning, 78, 92n3
synthetic views of language origins, 1

Tammet, Daniel, 44
time consciousness, 4, 101, 107, 133–37, 140–41, 147, 149; circadian clock, 133; cycles extending beyond a single generation, 140; as intervals, 133; as life span, 133; in physics, 133; as a rhematic symbol, 133;

umwelt, 14, 119, 126
Upper Paleolithic, 3, 23–29, 54, 63, 67–72, 84, 88–89, 91, 105–6, 108,

121–22, 125, 134–36, 138; diversity of artifact assemblages, 25, 123; emergent analytical capacities, 26, 105, 123; evidence for symbolism, 25–28, 50, 123; mobilary and parietal art, 50–53; propositional semiosis in, 29, 105; rhematic symbols in, 29, 50, 121; South African Upper Paleolithic, 3, 26; transition from Middle Paleolithic, 25–27. *See also* cave art; lithic technology
upright posture. *See* bipedalism

visual thinking, ix, 32, 36, 38, 42–48, 62, 70, 90, 121–22; as dominant mode of thought in non-human species, 81, 96, 101; in evolution of the brain, 72, 124; as iconicity and indexicality, 54, 80, 84, 86; as a manifestation of holistic processing, 63–64; in memory, 42–43, 63, 98–100; shift from visual to sequential thought, 69. *See also* autism; holistic thought
Vico, Giambattista, 107, 110n1
Von Petzinger, Genevieve, 29, 134, 144

Wargo, Melissa C., 18, 25
Washoe, 12, 17, 20n4
Williams, Donna, 34–37, 39
Wiltshire, Stephen, 37–39, 45
writing systems, 20, 126, 137–38, 143–46, 148

zoosemiosis, 96, 121; as species-specific cognitive manifestations, 97
zoosemiotics, 88, 96, 118, 120, 127n4

About the Authors

Karen A. Haworth holds a B.A. in anthropology from the University of Houston and an M.A. in psychology from the University of West Florida (UWF), and she worked as an office administrator in the Departments of Art and English at UWF. Her work on language origins includes scholarly essays and conference appearances over the past thirty years. She has been a member of the Language Origins Society and the Semiotic Society of America and has served as an editor for Semiotic Society publications. Since retirement, Karen has continued academic studies as an independent scholar.

Terry J. Prewitt is a retired professor, having taught and conducted research at the University of West Florida from 1981 through 2012. He began his career at the University of Houston and the University of Tulsa and was a visiting exchange professor at University College Dublin in 1986. He holds a B.A. in anthropology from San Diego State University and an M.A. and Ph.D. in anthropology from the University of Oklahoma, and he has been actively engaged in anthropological studies since the late 1960s. He has authored books, monographs, and articles on ethnography, archaeology, semiotics, anthropology of religion, and critical theory and served as a long-term executive director and editor for the Semiotic Society of America.

www.ingramcontent.com/pod-product-compliance
Lightning Source LLC
Chambersburg PA
CBHW052049300426
44117CB00012B/2040